also by David Falkner

Sadaharu Oh: A Zen Way of Baseball
(with Sadaharu Oh)

The Short Season: The Hard Work and High Times
of Baseball in the Spring

LT: LIVING ON THE EDGE

Lawrence Taylor

with

David Falkner

𝕿imes BOOKS

LT: LIVING ON THE EDGE

Library of Congress Cataloging-in-Publication Data

Taylor, Lawrence, 1959–
LT: living on the edge.

1. Taylor, Lawrence, 1959–   . 2. Football
players—United States—Biography. I. Falkner,
David.   II. Title.
GV939.T34A3 1987   796.332′982′4 [B]   87-9958
ISBN 0-8129-1703-0

Designed by Quinn Hall

Manufactured in the United States of America
9 8 7 6 5 4 3 2
First Edition

To my family and D'Fellas
—L.T.

For Hank Webb
—D.F.

Acknowledgments

The following people, each in an unmistakably individual and caring way, helped us in completing this book: Ricky Barden, David Black, Ivery Black, Glenn Carter, Bobby Cupo, Paul Davis, Byron Hunt, John Morning, Ed "Pee Wee" Olivari, Bill Parcells, Tom Power, Dylan Pritchett, Eric Pruden, Steve Rosner, Jerome Schwartz, Andrew Siff, Jenny Dowling Siff, Peter Skolnik, Clarence Taylor, Iris Taylor, Linda Taylor, and George Young. Special thanks to our editor, Jonathan Segal.

LT: LIVING ON THE EDGE

1

WHEN I was thirteen, I told my mama I would make a million dollars playing football by the time I was twenty-one.

I was off by a year.

I don't know why I said that to her. I was probably thinking of the million bucks—I was a runt of a kid then and made my spending money selling bootleg candy at school. But I believe I was born for football the way some people are born to be engineers or musicians.

In the NFL, being born for football doesn't guarantee you a thing. You've got to survive from game to game, from year to year. Teams don't put out hospital lists every week for nothing. The name of the game, no matter how much they pay you, is survival.

Last season opened with a loss in Dallas and ended with a win in the Super Bowl. You never plan on storybook seasons. You just play the game. The game is something so upspeed and uptempo you can't begin to describe it—it's in your body and you know it in the same way you know hunger or pain. Your life is on the line out there and you look forward to risking it rather than running away. You are crazy—and you can never explain why. I get so worked up before a game that I can barely keep my food down. I know what's out there. When the day comes that I let up and go out trying to watch my ass, that is the day something will happen and they will carry me out on the meat wagon.

It's always survival. Last season was different in that we went to the Super Bowl and I just happened to have cleaned some dope out of my system. (The two weren't necessarily connected.) I had the same game plan for all contingencies. It was simple: Do it on the field and to hell with the rest.

I spent the season playing and keeping my mouth shut. At Super Bowl time, I couldn't help myself. There were twenty-six hundred media people from twelve or thirteen different countries covering the game. You multiply that number by the number of dumb and irrelevant questions each single person has in them and you know you are likely to be playing King of the Hill on a pile of horseshit.

"LT? Do you think Denver is a really good team?"

"LT? What kind of quarterback is John Elway?"

"LT? Do you think there's too much hype around this game?"

No hype, guys, it's all football.

Hell, what are you going to do? I really didn't mind talking, especially after the season I'd had. But I had no doubts at all about what reporters would eventually want to ask me: "LT? Is the subject of your past too sensitive to talk about, or do you have a message about your comeback for America's youth?"

If I could just leave it with the old saying "To thine own self be true," that would be my message. But anyone in the public eye is playing to the expectations of other people— your words, your actions can be twisted.

Here's a question I got asked during hype week:

"LT? Can you describe what a sack really feels like?"

Roughly, I said this:

"It's when you have the chance to hit a quarterback when he doesn't see you coming and you drive your helmet into his back so hard he blows a little snot bubble out of his nose and the coach comes out and holds up three fingers and asks the quarterback 'How many?' and he says 'Seven.' "

A lot of papers covered that—but I didn't come across any that printed it quite as I said it. I'm not complaining, mind you. No doubt they were trying to shield me a little—protect my image or something. But hell, I wasn't looking to be shielded. I say what comes to mind. Things happen too fast on a football field to stop and analyze what you feel about them.

The point, though, isn't about quarterbacks' noses. It's about my life. I can't answer to other people's expectations. I cleaned some dope out of my system before last season. Everybody found out. LT's game's been off, you've seen him sleep in the locker room, drive his car like a lunatic—drugs, all along, were the reason. Just 2 and 2.

My game plan included not talking to people very much. I wasn't about to give people the satisfaction of saying your 2 and 2 are the numbers I play by. My number from day one in New York has been 56. All the way through last season, people would come up to me and say, "How're you doing?" They asked me that in training camp, they asked me that at the Super Bowl. I always knew what the question meant.

"I'm doing *fine*" was my usual answer. "How're *you* doing?"

I'm supposed to be a hero because football players are made into heroes. I'm no hero. I'm supposed to be a role model—whatever that means. I'm no role model. I live my life in the fast lane—and always have. I drink too much, I party too much, I drive too fast, and I'm hell on quarterbacks. It's always been that way. When somebody calls me crazy I take it as a compliment. I've always felt there was more to arithmetic than 2 and 2.

Pleasantville, New York, in the summer. Training camp, 1987. There's no Super Bowl in anyone's mind yet. It's hot and humid—not nearly as bad as back home in Virginia—

but hot and humid. There was that smell of football, that special, stomach-turning, funky smell of hard work and sweat.

"LT! LT! How're you doin'?"

"I'm doin' fine. How're *you* doin'?"

There are crowds every day baking their brains out in the bleachers next to the practice field. Afterward, they and the reporters line the gates in the parking lot. As soon as I get clear of them—whoosh, I gun my car like a rocket to get the hell out of there. Where am I going? Just to the dorm. Byron Hunt's got a cooler full of six-packs. I'll be back, back to the smell of it, back to what I have to do, back to my game plan.

I was told by the Giants' strength coach to lift weights this year. I've never been into weights. Don't like 'em, don't use 'em. But they think maybe I'll get stronger with them. Try 'em for a week or two. That's not in the game plan, though.

In the evening at Pleasantville, we eat a common meal and have meetings afterward. The players have time to walk around the pretty campus in their warm-up suits, saying hi and seeya later. There are women and businesspeople and media and God knows who else to let you know you never need to be alone in camp.

I made it clear right away that I wasn't going to be doing too much talking, never tried to hide it, never tried to be two-faced about it. I guess the word got around, because even business associates who needed to see me seemed a little edgy when I met them. They wanted to know if I was a serious or reliable person. Maybe they needed to know how I was doing, too? I don't know. What I do know is that I am a football player. And that's where it all goes down. I love the game of football. But from the time I was just a stick of a kid in Lightfoot, Virginia—population: general store, Baptist church, and a lot of trees—I've been the same person. Football hasn't changed me.

But last year I cleared some dope out of my system.

Once upon a time I chewed Red Man tobacco. I'd put it in bubble gum, stick it in my mouth so it had all kinds of extra juice in it, and I'd work on it till my jaws got tired. I could spit fifteen yards with that nasty load in there. It was a disgusting habit and sometimes I paid for it. I was a baseball catcher for many years. One time, I was catching a game—I was about eighteen—and a guy swung and fouled a ball right into my nuts. I automatically swallowed the wad I was chewing. I'm rolling around on the ground, grabbing here and grabbing there, my belly's on fire, my balls are gone, I thought I was gonna die on the spot. I didn't.

And I didn't quit chewing. Only changed brands.

Now I know how bad that stuff is, how harmful it is to your health. I sure don't want to get mouth cancer—but nobody will ever get me to stop by telling me I need to change my ways. I'm the only person who can do that for myself.

When I was in college, I had a friend, Steve Streater. He was my roommate for three years. Steve, like me, was a hell-raiser, real crazy—but we were the closest of friends, he was like a brother to me. He was from Sylvan, North Carolina, and his family back there became my second family. We did things together, went places together. Steve was a terrific athlete, all ACC (Atlantic Coast Conference) in football, the number one pick in baseball in the entire nation when he was in high school.

Steve had a car in college—and a lot of women. He was the guy to attach yourself to then, believe me. I told Steve right off, "Man, when you pull a woman, make sure she's got a friend." You would have had to see Steve to believe him. We'd drink and party all night. Then he'd get up the next morning and run all day. He was a punter, a free safety, and a free spirit. He talked like an old hillbilly, and everybody in my family knew him and loved him.

Just after I was drafted by the Giants and came up here for rookie camp, to meet the press, and so on—we were supposed to go to practice the following morning—I went out drinking half the night with Dave Young, a second-round draft pick that year. We'd gotten back around 2:30 or 3:00 A.M. and there was a call waiting for me in my room. It was my agent. He said, "LT, I've got some bad news for you. Steve has broken his neck."

I was so drunk and sleepy I didn't know what he was talking about.

"Steve *who*?" I said.

"Steve Streater," he said.

I don't remember what I said then. I know I just went berserk. I started screaming at the guy like it was *his* fault. I told him finally just to get me on the first flight out in the morning and to hell with the rest. It never even crossed my mind to tell the Giants I was going to leave camp.

When I was on my way out of the hotel to catch a 7:00 A.M. plane, I saw a guy from the Giants' office and told him that I was leaving and why. He said, "Lawrence, I think you should talk to the coach."

"To hell with that," I said. "Fuck football." And I left.

I got to the airport in Carolina and my girlfriend—now my wife, Linda—was there and we went straight to the hospital. Right up to the moment I got to the lobby of that hospital, I swore I was going to keep my cool so Steve could see that everything was going to be all right. But as soon as I saw that place, I got this feeling in my stomach—I didn't want to go in. I was afraid to. I didn't want to go in there and see him.

When I finally got up enough courage and went inside, his parents were sitting quietly by his bed. What really broke me up, though, was the doctor. I saw him first—and he told me that Steve had been asking for me. I guess they had all just gotten back from the emergency room.

Then I saw Steve.

He was wearing something that looked like a crown on his head. There were metal bolts in his skull. I stood next to him and all I could say—like some dumb fool—was, "Steve, it's going to be all right."

Tears were coming out of his eyes.

The doctor—Dr. Taft—came up to me and whispered that Steve was going to be paralyzed. It was like something snapped inside. I pushed him into a corner and started yelling at him.

"You're a damned doctor and you tell me you can't do anything for him?"

I'm raving at him. I didn't know what I was doing.

I calmed down but I didn't apologize. I talked to Steve's parents. He had been in a car crash. He had been to Washington where he said the Redskins had signed him and on his way home there had been an accident—caused by what I don't know. His car went off the road.

I didn't want to play football anymore. I stayed at the hospital with Steve all day and then sat up with him all night, finally going to sleep in his room. I never felt so bad—before or since—in my life.

I thought about dying. I had been in trouble in my life, thought maybe this or that would kill me—but it was nothing compared to this.

Steve was my boy.

He told me finally to go out there and live my life, do my best. I did that. I told Steve one day that I was gonna go back and play football and that that season—my first with the Giants—would be for him.

I had a great rookie year.

Today Steve works for an organization that campaigns against drunk driving—and sometimes I go down there and make appearances to help him out. When he comes up here, sometimes he'll sit around in his wheelchair when we play basketball—and I'll treat him the same all the time. I'll tease him, "Hey, why don't you jump out of that chair and come on out here and play some basketball?" Steve is the bravest guy I've ever met in my life, and as much as I feel for him, I could never actually begin to know what he's gone through.

But my life is the same. I don't know if we're here to

learn from people or just to stand by them. I'll stand by Steve for as long as we're both alive—because he's who he is.

I often think about what happened to him—a guy who seemed to have everything, only to have it all shattered before his life had really gotten started.

I think about death sometimes. I'm not particularly afraid of it. A long time ago I read a poem about an athlete dying young—I don't know who wrote it, but I remember feeling that if you ever did die young, when everything was going really well, that wouldn't be so bad. It would be better than getting old and watching the flowers grow.

It's true that my life is out there in the fast lane. Nobody has to point out consequences for me, because I've seen them as close up as any human being could. But my priorities are mine and no one else's. And so is my way of looking at things.

I do some things you would not believe. I live out there on the edge—back of the line on Sundays and a few other places the rest of the time. New York City is the biggest playground in the world. I've been in the penthouses and the gutters. I hang out with names and with bums. Sometimes in the middle of the night I'll sit on street corners with homeless people. They have names, too. I'm no better than they are, they are just as human as I am.

I met a guy down home one day after I had become a big star. This guy thought he was Jesus Christ and the cops were about to bust him and haul him off to jail or the nuthouse. His family was sitting in a car by the curb watching what was going on. The car, it turned out, was the only home they had. This guy—Jesus Christ—was saying that if only they had the money to get to Chicago, everything would be all right. I gave the guy and his family the money, a few thousand bucks, to go. I wasn't better than they were—just happened to have enough money in my pocket. It was no big deal. Anybody who has ever read his Bible knows that the real Jesus Christ knew misery, and also something about rich people being no better than poor people.

But my game is football. I play it because I love it, because I was lucky enough to be given a talent for it.

I want to be the meanest sonuvabitch who ever played. I want to be the best.

But then there's this stuff about drugs. There's what really happened and then there's what people think. One is easier to deal with than the other. I didn't kill anybody; I took some drugs. There's an epidemic out there—and so in my position it gets to the point where I can't even piss into a bottle without its being some sort of circus act. Some of my coaches will say "Where are you going, LT?" I'll tell 'em, "I'm going to get cocaine. You want to come?"

I'm the same person I always was.

I was never this ideal football hero people wrote about Before the Fall—or the other kind they were looking for but didn't find at Super Bowl time.

The person who knows best about the man in the mirror is me. I came into 1986 with my own game plan. I didn't need to answer to anyone, because first I was going to answer to myself. There are things I had to say to my family and friends—and to football. They have already been said. And then I was going to tell my story in my way.

I know where I come from, and I know what happened.

I wasn't born with a silver spoon in my mouth and a football in my hand. In fact, I didn't start playing football till my sophomore year in high school—and then it wasn't even for my school team. When I was growing up, I didn't watch football, didn't follow it on TV or in the papers.

Out where I lived, not too much happened. There was a two-lane highway that ran past our house, which was set back in the woods beyond a steep gulley. Our closest neighbors were across the other side of the road. There were neighbors on our side, too, but you had to go up through the woods to find them.

I had very little contact with other people growing up. I spent a lot of early time with baby-sitters and then, later, because my folks always wanted to know where their children were, spent most of my time outside school at home. Because school was the only place I could really socialize, my attendance record was perfect from grade school right on through high school.

I think all the hours I spent alone help explain why I still don't feel at ease today being surrounded by too many people.

I was one of three boys, the middle one, each of us a year apart. We were each other's company for quite a while—and we did what brothers do in a tight family. We played and fought and conspired and vied against each other and stood up for one another. We were rambunctious kids—I was far more so than Buddy and Kim. I figured out devices to get them to do my chores—my folks left us lots to do—and I was always quick with plans and energy. I was wild from the start.

My mom says that when I was eight, my brothers and I tackled a cop and I took away his gun.

I don't remember that. I do remember getting in a fight with my older brother, Buddy, once and getting so mad that I took a kitchen knife and flung it at him. It whistled past his ear and stuck right in the wall quivering like something out of an old Western movie.

My mom and pop were the closest people in our lives. They both worked and scrimped for everything we had. My pop worked in the shipyards at Newport News, Virginia, and still does. And my mom had all kinds of low-paying jobs, cashier and clerk in a five-and-dime, check-out person in a Laundromat. We didn't get to see them too much because they worked so hard and so long, but the time we did have with them was precious.

I remember getting up every morning at four-thirty when my pop got up for work. Either he'd wake me or I'd wake up first. Sometimes I'd slide into bed next to my folks; nearly all the time I'd go into the kitchen to have breakfast with my father. I ate oatmeal with him every morning because he loved oatmeal. I hated oatmeal—but it was a chance to be with my pop.

My mom was probably the closest person in my life then. She not only looked after me, it was also like she was a guiding spirit, a friend, and a disciplinarian at the same time. No matter how hard she worked, she always had time for her children, loving time, talking time. She'd put the dishes off till later so she could read us nursery rhymes at night. And on Fridays, when her workweek was over, she'd get us to turn the TV off and pull up chairs around the kitchen table so we could spend the evening talking—about anything that was on our minds. She taught us to be God-fearing, to make something of ourselves, to believe in ourselves. She wanted us all to go to college because she believed if we didn't we'd face a life of minimum wages—and from our talks, when we all dreamed together about what we wanted to be, it was clear to all of us that the life-styles we wanted—like most people—couldn't be had on minimum wages.

Both my folks were old-fashioned in their sense of discipline. They had us work hard around the house and at school. If we stepped out of line, they didn't spare the belt or the birch. My pop was a quiet type, didn't talk all that much, but when he got mad, look out. My mom was no pushover, either. She was on to everything we did. Because we came from a small town where everybody knew everybody, her intelligence about her children was amazing. You might think you got away with something, but you never did. I don't know how many times, she'd tell me, "Lonnie, get on out in the yard and pick me a switch."

I'd nearly always bring her back one with the leaves still on and she'd nearly always have me strip them before she used it on me.

I got to be afraid of my pop for a while because in the hardness of his life, he seemed to withdraw and come out of it only in anger. There was a period of time in my teens when I thought he might actually lash out and kill me.

But I was the kind of kid who was going to do his own thing no matter what. I'd test any rules that were set down for me. You tell me no, I'll try yes. If something seems impossible or too difficult, I'll say it's possible and probably could be made easier. I drove my parents crazy.

I remember being flat broke, absolutely without pocket money once. To overcome that, I forged a check of my mother's, took it to the country store up the road where we did our shopping, and paid our family's monthly bill with it.

I made out the check for a few dollars over so I could have something for myself. With that extra money, I bought piles of junk candy—Blow Pops, Bazookas, you name it—and re-sold them in school for a profit. I paid my mother back and never was without pocket money after that. They wound up calling me "Candy Man" in school. There were times where I even wound up lending my mother money for the movies.

My pop came home with a bicycle one day. I wanted to try it out. None of us was allowed to. My pop had this thing about all his vehicles, including this bike—they were *his*. He was especially crazy about his cars. We'd get to wax and wash them three times a week till we wanted to run and hide in the woods. He'd mark his vehicles in the dirt by the tires to make sure nobody would ever move them when he wasn't around.

Well, one day when he wasn't there, I borrowed his bike. I jumped on it and rode it downtown to Williamsburg, three miles away. When I got there I took it over a curb. Disaster. I not only blew a tire on that bad boy but wound up crushing the wheel as well.

I didn't know what to do. There wasn't a bike shop around and I couldn't lug the thing around on my back. In-stead, I tossed the wreckage into some underbrush behind a friend's house and beat it home in a panic.

When my pop came home and saw that his bike was gone, he naturally got steamed. But he couldn't blame any-one because he didn't know anything. I suggested that maybe the bike had been stolen when no one was home. I know he suspected me, but he couldn't prove a thing.

The next day, when he went off to work, I finally had worked out a plan. I stole his truck. I didn't know how to drive the damn thing—I was only eleven years old—but I was able to get it into first gear and steer it from our yard all the way downtown. My intention was to pick up the bike and drive it around to different mechanics till I found one who would fix it. I'd get the bike repaired and the truck back and on its marks all before my pop returned from work. It was a great plan, a daring plan—except for one thing:

The truck broke down at high noon in the middle of the busiest street in Williamsburg—and right in front of an aunt of mine who just happened to be passing by. I pleaded with her not to say a word of this to my father—she didn't—and then I set out to find a mechanic.

I eventually found someone willing to help. He confirmed my worst fears. I had turned the truck into scrap iron. The motor had literally blown up under the strain I had put on it. He towed the truck back to our yard and even inched the thing up to its marks in the dirt. Then—and only then—I told him the next part of my sad story:

I didn't have the money to pay him. To keep him from telling my dad, I think I might have promised him my life. Instead the guy was willing to settle for my promise to mow his lawn that Saturday. It turned out the guy wasn't just operating out of the kindness of his heart. When I showed up at his house, I saw that his lawn was two acres wide. He gave me a push mower and told me to have a good time.

Anyway, I had successfully schemed my way out of big trouble. My pop didn't look at his truck for two days after I got it back in place and then, when he did, he wound up cursing General Motors instead of me.

If I sound a little hard on my pop, I don't mean to be. My father and mother were both married at a very young age—he was twenty, she was eighteen. Neither of them had had any real experience of the world or even of that ordinary time of being young and carefree.

My pop was raised by his grandmother—whom we all called "Big Mama"—up the road in Toano, about ten miles from where we lived. All through my childhood, we'd take Sunday drives up there to be with his kinfolk. He played softball there for a team called the Toano Giants. And the Giants had a left fielder everyone called Bugs Bunny. Bugs

Bunny had two kids—J.P. and O'Brien—who became early playmates of mine.

My pop was raised by his grandmother because his real mother had him very young and left him in his grandmother's care so she could go off and find work in the East. My daddy's father, who loved him a lot, had a hard time finding work, drank a lot, and finally was shot by a woman he had been seeing, dying soon afterward. For years, my pop used to drive his father and his buddies around when they went drinking. They treated my pop real well, they all had a good time together, but my pop came away feeling that he wanted his own life to be a lot less wild than that. He vowed to find a good job when he got out of school—and then he got married and took on responsibilities he was really too young for. He had somehow missed his own youth in the process.

Years later, after I had joined the Giants, my pop and I went for a drive one day and he told me about his life. I saw him very differently after that. I was old enough and secure enough to understand him for the first time.

My pop was also sports crazy. He was short—five foot eight—and he had always told himself his height prevented him from having a pro career. But he was a good baseball player, good at basketball, at anything athletic. He'll still get me up in the morning to run with him when I go home. He leaves me looking for shortcuts after a couple of miles.

What he couldn't have in the way of a career, he got as a fan. He was particularly into football. He'd watch high school games, college games, and on Sundays in our house, he'd clear out the TV room so he could watch the one o'clock game, the four o'clock game, and, if there was one, the nine o'clock game, too. He always tried to get his kids to watch with him—just as he always wanted us to go out and shoot hoops with him. My brothers were more into watching with him than I was; from day one I was into the action part of all sports but not the listening and watching parts. Later on, when I became a football player myself, my pop's watching and knowledge became something else. To this day, when he says something about the game, I listen—because he knows what he's talking about.

"Lawrence," he'll tell me, "there were only a couple of guys around that fumble. The name of the game is football, which means the action takes place where the ball is."

I'll look at my pop and say, "I just heard that from Belichick this morning!"

My mom thinks my pop would have been a great coach.

The thing about both my parents is that old-fashioned and strict as they were, they held a family together and were there for their children. As difficult as we got, they did their best—which is all you can ever hope for. They were determined always to keep their children on a straight path to a good and honest life.

When we were very young, my brothers and I regularly were sent to church and Sunday school. I've always been grateful for that—no matter how far I've strayed. The Bible stories I heard then, I remember today; they are part of me. I love and remember the singing and can still hear my own voice saying prayers when I later became a junior deacon. I can still see the three of us walking up through the woods in our Sunday best on our way to church, holding hands.

Later on, when I began to slip as far as religion was concerned, I still regularly went to church choir. Then it was mainly because the prettiest girls in James City County were there—but I still loved the singing and the feeling it gave me. That whole early experience is still a guide for me, something I try to remember even in the midst of my wildest times.

There are guys on the Giants today—George Martin, for one—who are deeply religious. I don't make fun of them. I keep hoping to learn from them.

My folks guided me toward everything they thought

would make my life easier and better—church, school, and later on, college.

But maybe because of all the time I spent alone—or just because I was born that way—I always had this sense of being independent, of wanting to do things for myself. I was curious and eager to find out about the world outside my home. More than anything, you can just say I was curious. It turns out that was what led me to football—quite literally.

One day, when I was fifteen, I was at baseball practice at a local diamond. Baseball was my first love then. On an adjoining field, the Williamsburg Jaycee football team was working out. The coach over there thought I was a good athlete and asked me if I wanted to come out for his team. I didn't want to but I found out that once a year this team exchanged visits with another Jaycee team from Pittsburgh. The schedule that year called for a game in Pittsburgh. That was enough for me.

I joined the Jaycee team right afterward. The idea of going all the way to Pittsburgh, without parental supervision, seemed too good to be true—I wasn't about to miss it.

Small as I was, I became a good player for the Jaycees. The coach, Pete Babcock, was a guy who put this program together single-handedly. He paid some big-shot golfer to come down and do a benefit from which he raised enough money to outfit a boys' football team—which he ran. He told me from the start that I was going to play linebacker—and that was just fine with me. I knew I didn't want to be a defensive lineman and I never had any thought of being a quarterback because there were no black quarterbacks on real football teams. Linebacker was quarterback on defense because you controlled the game from there and you had to use your mind.

I got books out from the school library on linebackers. I read a lot of stuff about Ray Nitschke and Jack Ham and Sam Huff. What I read was how they saw the game, what their feeling was, what their tempo was. I got this concept right then that aside from being smart, a good linebacker was also a mean sonuvabitch.

I knew I was wild, but I wasn't mean at all back then. I told myself, however, that that was what I *could* be like. That was for me.

I didn't become mean in that year with the Jaycees—or through most of the next year, when I was playing for Lafayette, my high school. Going out for the Jaycees really meant taking a trip to Pittsburgh. I didn't really care about much else.

The day came and we actually made the trip.

It was late November or early December—I don't remember exactly—and it took us almost seven hours to drive there. We went in individual cars; I was in a group with five or six other players.

I don't remember the final score of the game—it might have ended in a tie—but it was hard-fought and I know we got our butts kicked. I do remember there was snow on the ground when we played. I had never played football in the snow before—or afterward, save for one time in the pros.

What I remember most was the trip itself. There weren't a whole lot of blacks on our team or theirs. We stayed with the families of the players on the other team, and there were about six of us who stayed with this one white family who had three players on the Pittsburgh Jaycees. That was fine with me. I had played and been friends with whites all the way through Little League and Pony League. I think sports, more than anything, was why I never got too worked up about the black thing when I was in school or afterward. Anyway, this family was as nice as could be to us. They let us watch TV when we wanted and they let us come and go as we pleased.

I walked all around the town, as far as I could go. Everything seemed so different. There were so many hills and all the houses and streets seemed part of these hills. I walked up and down hour after hour till it was late at night. I saw kids tearing along on skateboards and the day turning gray like steel behind them. Looking down from the hills into the city, you could just tell it was a steel town, a hard town. You knew that people who lived in this city, lived and died hard. Whatever they did, whether it was football or anything else, they did it hard. All the guys looked stocky and hard—and the women looked the same.

I had an amazing time staying with that family. Those folks even had a different language. I remember one day sitting around after dinner feeling very thirsty. For about four or five hours before that, I had been thirsty, too, and the father of these kids kept asking me, "Do you want any pop?" I felt weird because I thought he was talking about "pot." All day long, I kept saying, "No. No, thank you." I must have said "no, thank you" more that day than any time in my life. Finally, late at night, he said to me, "Are you sure you don't want any pop? We've got grape and orange, we've got Coke, we've got Dr Pepper." I said, "Yeah, I'll take one. I'll take three." I guess it was funny. I told my friend's mom that I hadn't understood the word "pop," and they all got to laughing hard.

I didn't mind. I was thirsty.

You could say that's the way my football career began.

Years later, when I was a rookie linebacker on the Giants, the veteran linebackers on the team teased me all the time because I didn't know one NFL city from another. Brad Van Pelt and Brian Kelley came up to me just before we made a road trip to Seattle in that first season.

"Taylor," they said, "better take your mud cleats. It rains a lot in Seattle."

I emptied my equipment bag of all my turf shoes and put in my cleats.

I didn't know Seattle played in a domed stadium.

The truth of the matter is I didn't know much about anyplace beyond where I lived. For years, that was just my own house—then it was school, then a college town, then a huge metropolis and a whole country.

Yet the ironic thing is that I've really never left home. When I most need to get in touch with who I am, I know where to go. My folks and my hometown aren't distant memories for me. Last June, when all the Super Bowl awards and banquets were done, I went back to Williamsburg for the tenth anniversary of my high school class.

It meant more to me than anything.

SOMETIMES, if I know the press isn't looking, I go out to high schools in the New York metropolitan area and talk to kids whose teachers believe football stars might help set them straight. I don't believe in setting anyone else straight—I have a hard enough time with myself—and I can't begin to say what I see when I get to most of these schools. Big-city life is too crowded, too run-down, too split apart and impersonal. Never mind foreign aid, I want to say, get some help here on the home front. And then I think about my own school, Lafayette. I was lucky.

It was the only high school in Williamsburg, and there was no problem of segregation or busing because whites and blacks, from the start, shared the same place, whether they liked it or not. And because the Burg was small enough, people knew each other. You could spend time at sports or playing tag with your cars in the middle of the night with your friends—till the police stopped you; you could drink a ton of beer and sit out half the night at the railroad bridge in Mooretown, a couple of miles away, bullshitting about everything—till some neighbors complained. But you'd always be known by name, and there was no trouble in any of it.

Lafayette, which was about four miles by bus from my house, was just another extention of home.

I wasn't a great student, but I kept at it—I did what I had

to—and I might have been better if football hadn't finally come along. When I went out for football at Lafayette in my junior year, I still wasn't sure I wanted to. There was no trip to Pittsburgh at the end of the high school season.

In my sophomore year, one of the assistant coaches at school, Melvin Jones—he's the head coach now—got ahold of me and said, "Come here, son, let's talk."

He reminded me that if you were black and came from a small town in the South and you wanted to go to college and get ahead, you had better think about things like football. If you were black and from the rural South, you thought about football the way other kids thought about careers in law or medicine.

I told him then I wasn't interested in playing for Lafayette, that I was going to play for the Jaycees.

He told me playing for the Jaycees was little league.

Coach Jones recently related the next step in the story to some friends of mine:

"When I told Taylor, 'Why don't you stand up for your school?' he said, 'Nah, I'm playin' down there.' Down there Taylor played his own game, he wasn't disciplined. I went down to the Jaycees a while ago—they wanted me to talk to them. Got there a little early so I could see what was going on. Saw one young man get tackled and he took all day getting up. When he finally got to his feet he threw the ball at the guy who hit him—threw it real hard. Then he came back and the coaches took him by the arm and he pulled away. I'm talking about little league, you see. I looked when they came off the field. They sat on their helmets. I thought: 'Behavior.' I knew what I was going to talk about. 'Behavior.' You get off your helmets. Discipline. One guy said, 'I don't have to listen to you, I'm not going to Lafayette, I'm going to Boone next year.' I said, 'I don't care if you're going to hell next year, you will listen to me.' Talking about 'Pride.' Yeah, you had a good time, yeah, you won a championship, but it's little league. Newspapers don't cover it. They call in the results. Told that to Taylor. Gonna get your name in the news-papers. Your school's no little league."

Coach Melvin Jones is like a cross between Vince Lom-bardi and the Reverend Jesse Jackson. There are inspirational sayings all over the walls of his office. He wears a big button that says, "Proud to Be a Teacher." Whenever he gets one going, he just naturally breaks into rhyme, you know. "If you can perceive it and believe it, then you can achieve it!" Look out for Coach Jones!

Anyway, it finally got to be impossible to avoid football. For one thing, I had gotten into the habit of playing sandlot at school. Every lunch break since I had been to Lafayette, I used to go out and play tackle football. We played without equipment and we played hard for about thirty-five or forty-five minutes. You got so sweaty and dirty and foul-smelling that when you went to your next class, everybody knew what you had been doing. Lafayette was a new school—I was in the first class that spent a full four years there—and the place was built funny. It had no windows. The whole school, except for the principal's office, had no windows. One way in and one way out of any classroom—people and smells got sealed in, for better or worse. People knew me—by my smell—as a football player before I actually was one!

Anyway, I kept hearing it from Coach Jones and others: Was I gonna go out for football? When was I gonna go out and stand up for my school? I could have told them that I was getting around to it because I had gone to enough pep rallies on the nights before the games and I knew the cheer-leaders and all the pretty girls in the school seemed to show along with lots of other people. You could always tell who the football players were because they wore their uniform jerseys to the rallies and they just stood out. The excitement just seemed to build and build.

But if you had asked me back then whether or not I tried out because I had gotten to the point of calculating a college or pro career, the answer is no—it was there in the back of my head, but mainly I was thinking this might be a way to have a good time. Lafayette had a strong football team. I didn't know if I could make the squad.

I worked hard. I had a lot to make up for because I had already missed two years. I was 5-7 or 5-8 and weighed no more than 180. Though Lafayette didn't have a big team, there were plenty of linemen over 200 pounds, and I got hit hard so many times, I felt like I was going to get wiped out before I ever wound up in a game. When the season started, I was deep on the bench and my body was sore all over. One time, before the season opened, I took one hit too many in practice and told myself, "That's it. I quit." I started off the field, heading for the locker room. When I did that, Coach Jones was right behind me. This was a piece of luck.

He was angry.

"Where you going?" he said.

"I'm going in," I said.

"I am too," he said, "but I'm bringing your ass back."

"I can't handle this!"

"Yes you can!" He was at his preacher best. You could see his chest puffing out and the fire sirens going off in his head.

"You made a commitment," he shouted, "and it said nothin' about walkin' away!" He clapped his hands real loud. "It said, *you got to finish!* And you're going to stay here this year and do it and I don't care if they beat your ass all over the field!"

I don't know whether it was then or later that I told Coach Jones that I didn't know if I was equal to some of the other players on the team. He told me, "You're a black player. You want to be equal, then be twice as good! That's equality!"

I went back out there because I thought I had to. I began to see what this Coach Jones was about. I mean, once I *had* made this commitment to the team, Coach Jones was there to enforce it—and he was an enforcer. He also taught a con-struction class. He taught his students to build a whole house from the foundations up. He was into building things, including kids.

To tell the truth, I wasn't quite ready to be built into anything by anyone in those days. Back then, for example, everyone used to wear big ole Afros. I had one, and like a lot of other people, I was always wanting to plait it into tight little braids. Now, Coach Jones—and my father—had no use for this. I had to really watch myself and make sure I plaited only when I thought I could get away with it. Coach Jones had a squad of guys from his construction class who went around with these rake combs, which were long and could be sharpened into weapons. These guys were real goons. If they found you with a plait, they were on orders from Coach Jones to rake your hair out on the spot. If these guys ever hit you in the head with one of their rakes, you could be in serious physical trouble. After I went out for football, the only time I could plait was just before I got on the school bus going home—and then I had to rake out my hair before my pop got home. But I did it. It made no sense but I was a rebel by instinct as much as I was a football player.

Now most of my time on the field was practice time. And it left me constantly wondering what I was doing. I must have asked myself a million times why I was really doing this. Aside from getting my butt kicked, I wasn't play-ing. You have these twice-a-day workouts. At the end of the summer and the beginning of fall in Virginia it's as hot and humid as a swamp. You run these gassers up and down the field, do these damn little drills—and always there's this smell of football. Football has such a distinct smell. If you were held incommunicado and blindfolded in someone's house and then were led outside, not knowing where you were going, and taken to a football field, you'd know where you were right away just from the stomach-turning stench of it. I hated it then, but today that smell just means hard work.

When the games came, I'd sit on the bench, scared shitless and praying that I wouldn't be sent in.

My mom and pop were excited, of course, by my being on the football team, especially my pop. He used to tell me the same stuff as Coach Jones about staying with it—he didn't care if I went out and got my ass fractured just as long as he could see that I was willing to go back out there the next day.

And I did. And after a while, my body started getting used to the abuse. And I started to enjoy what I was doing. It meant something to be able to take it—and then pay back some—from guys who had played for that long and who were regularly tattooing me.

By the time the season began, I felt like I had started to get my timing down. I wasn't fast then—my speed couldn't have been more than 4.9—but I was probably football fast. I got shifted around from defensive end to tackle to guard and center. Once I stopped being fresh meat out there, I could feel myself learning from week to week.

But I was definitely second team, and though I reached a point where I kept telling myself that I just wanted the chance to get into the game and play, I was content to be sitting there talking to myself about all the great things I could do if I ever got into the game.

Then in the fifth game of the season, everything changed. We were playing our archrival, Bethel, at home on a Friday night at Cooley Field. It was the second quarter, second series of plays. The score was tied, 0–0, and Bethel was moving on us. Our defensive end, Tony McConnel, was getting killed. Bethel was just driving play after play at him, and the only way they were going to be stopped was if they fumbled or messed up in some other way. At one point on this drive, they ran a long gain right around Tony's end. The coach said—I can still hear his voice, just like in the movies—"Taylor, get ready!" Sure. Eight to ten thousand people

screaming their heads off, my mom and pop in the stands—
what a bullshit artist I had been. Getting into the game was
the last thing I wanted! Now my coach is telling me, "Get out
there!" Oh, man, I wanted to throw up. I wasn't about to
show it to anyone, but I was sick to my stomach and shaking
all over. I was so scared it was unreal. The difference between my nerves then and now is that when I go out there
today, I know who I am as a football player. I won't let anyone see that I'm nervous—because that might get to them,
too.

Once I got into that first game, I made a couple of plays.
I started chasing people left and right, chasing them down. I
made a few stops when they came at me. It must have looked
funny because I was such a roly-poly kid and my body went
in all different directions. Little butterball with arms and
legs flying out this way and that—every part of my body was
in motion. My nerves were fine—it was raining and cold and
on every tackle you went slipping and sliding in the mud. I
loved every minute of it!

I made a lot of tackles as the evening wore on. I played
well and I knew it. We hit the last quarter and the score was
still tied at 0–0. We got down to the last minute of the game
and Bethel had just run three plays deep in its own territory
and was forced to kick.

On this last play, Tony McConnel was lined up on the
outside and I was inside. The assignment we all had was
simple: Just rush. Our punt-return team was in place, everybody knew what they had to do, the ball was snapped, and
all I remember then was crashing and leaping. They were
backed up in their own zone, and when I leaped, I blocked
their punt. The ball went straight up in the air and it came
down right in Tony McConnel's hands—he recovered it for a
touchdown, and we won the game, 6–0.

Everyone went wild, the players, the town. Bethel was
our biggest game and they nearly always were in contention
to win the state title every year.

I remember afterward, the excitement just continued. We were all so happy. A few players and I loaded into a car, and we went barreling down the road. We stopped at the first 7-Eleven we could find and I bought some Mad Dog 20/20 and lots of Miller beer. In those days, you could get a big ole bottle of Mad Dog—Mogen-David wine—for seventy-nine cents. The guys in front had a bottle, and we had one in the back.

I worked on my Miller for a while, then I got around to the Mad Dog. Hell, I wasn't really into drinking then—drank some beer and nothing else—but I was too happy to worry. I kept working on the Mad Dog. We were on our way to a party and I kept guzzling away. We were gonna have some fun, we were gonna party till we dropped.

By the time I got to this party, which was at a real fancy house where one of the players lived, my head was buzzing. I remember coming up to the porch of this house already feeling a little funny and there was this big, mean-looking German shepherd dog barking at us as we went up the steps. Anyway, when I got inside, I just had to sit down. And as soon as I sat down, my head began to get real light. I was not feeling well at all. After a minute or two I got up. I didn't see the people around me, I wasn't thinking of anything but just getting outside again. I went out and got as far as the carport before I threw up.

I got on my hands and knees and kept throwing up everywhere. I never felt so sick in my life. And just then this dog comes squaring around the corner—mean, mean, mean—barking as loud as he could, running right up to me. I was so sick I didn't even care. This dog could have been a wolf that hadn't had a meal in a week and I wouldn't have moved. He looked at me, I looked at him, and I just kept throwing up. The dog finally came over to me, but when he got there he stopped short and began sniffing. He turned and walked off. If you had seen this move it was like the dog saying out loud, "I think I'll just leave this one alone."

The party was over for me. The guys had to take me home. It was raining and raining and all the time I had my head out the window throwing up on the car as it went. We had to stop about four or five times so I could throw up some more.

When they finally got me home, they let me out on the top of the road leading down into the woods before my house. I didn't want them to drive all the way in because I didn't want my parents alerted. I got out on the side of the road, the guys drove off, I took two steps forward, and then fell flat on my face. I rolled all the way down the hill, through underbrush and mud and dead branches. I rolled as far as I could go. And then I just lay there with the rain beating on my face. I could hear cars passing by above me. The rain just kept hitting my face and I was too sick to move. I started praying. I prayed that God would give me just enough strength to get me to the house, and I prayed, above all, that my mother wouldn't find out. Then I had another prayer: "Dear God, just let me die."

My eyes were burning, my mouth felt like cotton, I didn't feel the rain, and I don't think if anybody asked me then I could have told them my name. But here was a preview of my game—wildness on the field and wildness off it—success right on the edge of things. One step this way, glory. One step the other—forget it! I've been trying to keep the two in balance ever since.

Somehow I managed to crawl to the house. I got inside and dragged a trash can next to my bed. Then I fell down on my mattress and blacked out. The next morning my mom got me out of bed early to do chores. She didn't need any clues to figure things out. She said nothing, but she made me work my butt off. I had a splitting headache but I did all the chores I was supposed to do—and by the time I finished I was actually feeling a little bit better.

It was Saturday afternoon and I decided to go downtown. By then the papers were out and my name was all over the sports pages. People were saying hello and congratulations and clapping me on the back. I found out why. I picked up a paper and there it all was, in print. I couldn't believe my eyes. My name was in the papers for something good that I had done! I wanted to run all the way home and show my folks. Wanted to tell them something: Hey, I'm on my way!

4

FROM that Bethel game in the middle of my junior year, right through to the end of my senior year, I played one good football game after another. I never returned to the bench, never again found myself hoping that I wouldn't be sent into play. For the first time I was really good at something. And there was no way I was going to let that go.

I made up for lost learning time with each game I played. We had a good coaching staff, five coaches in all, all who had had football experience of one kind or another. I learned a lot on my own, too. I "thought" myself into other players, players on my own team, players on opposing teams. I do that today—I feel my way into the quarterback's skin so that I almost know his moves before he does. It's natural, and you learn from it by going with it. I learned what the coaches had to show me about different blocks and the like—nothing went in one ear and out the other—but I learned most from football situations. What are they going to do here? If I was in their shoes, where would I go, what would I do? It was like my thinking and my body worked simultaneously.

My folks wanted me to go to college at that point, but we had no money. A football scholarship was almost the only way I could have gone. I didn't think about it seriously till then. (I really don't move on anything till the last minute when my back is to the wall and the pressure is most intense. I prefer a big game to a "soft" one for that reason. I deal with crises in my life—like drugs—the same way; last split second, when I'm right on the edge, my whole system on red alert.)

It wasn't at all clear that I was going to get offered very much because I had started so late in my junior year, after most college scouts had been through Williamsburg and seen our team.

Coach Jones tried to get schools interested in me after that—especially as I had this phenomenal spurt of growth over that summer. I went from being 5-8 and 180 to 6-1 and 205. Coach Jones'd yell at these guys on the phone, "Come up here, come up and look at the film, come look at 89, he's a *ballplayer!*"

Coach Jones had once played for the Bears. He used that with the recruiters, too. "I saw Dick Butkus play," he'd say. "Now, Butkus was *crazy*—he looked vicious. He was so mean they could put him in a cage, his eye was that *cold*. Well, that's what Taylor has in his eye . . . you want him bigger, come up here and take the boy out to Hardee's or McDonald's, I'm talkin' about a *ballplayer!*"

I think God and a hard lifting job over the summer helped my body, but Coach Jones may have helped even more with his persistence and his belief in me. I wasn't about to let him—or myself—down.

At the end of my junior year, there had been some talk in a few papers about my being a possible All-State candidate. In my senior year I eventually won honors as an outside linebacker or defensive end and then also as a tight end on offense. I had a helluva year. The offers I did get were in long before the end of the season.

I loved playing defense, of course, but that one year of playing on offense—oh, that was sweet. Bill Parcells recently told a couple of people that he thinks I could still be an outstanding offensive player in the NFL. I'd never call him on that. My luck from the start has been that my coaches constantly steered me to outside linebacking. But I know that year of pass catching taught me a lot.

Of course I remember the first touchdown pass I caught—I can still see it coming, still remember thinking, "Just don't drop the sonuvadog," still feel the ball hitting my hands. But what I took away from that, which carried over into my defensive play, was getting this feel for what was around me.

Receivers and linebackers both have this sense of what's in the neighborhood. You get a visual on the field without having to go over everything in detail. It's like when you cut this way, you see everything in a flash, you get a picture of where everybody is, and when the ball comes you're able to stay concentrated on it—because the toughest part of being a pass catcher is mental, not physical. It's staying absolutely concentrated in traffic when your back is to the guy who wants to turn you into spare ribs. It's like that for defensive players, too. You get this speed flash on a pass play, so you automatically know that a ball is going to a certain place and what impact there's going to be afterward. Because I've been able to "see" this way, I've almost never had pass interference called on me in the pros. Another way of thinking about this kind of "seeing" is to imagine a dark room—you enter it blind but you somehow know if someone else is in the room.

I wasn't "heavily" recruited. I got offers from two schools I seriously considered: the University of Richmond and the University of North Carolina. There were a number of small schools that wrote me letters—I showed them proudly to my friends—but I was never interested.

I chose North Carolina for a number of reasons. It was a big school, it was away from home, and doing well there would make it easier to get to the pros.

I also liked the Tar Heels' recruiter, Mike Mansfield. I've met a lot of different recruiters by now, but Mike Mansfield was the best. He was a no-bullshit friend all the way. His interest in me continued even after I entered the school; I never had the feeling at any point that he was laying it on just to impress me. He didn't come on with phony promises or little hidden things under the table. He was an impressive-looking guy, a considerate person who listened, answered all the questions I had, my family had, and genuinely tried to make things easier for me.

My one visit to Carolina in my senior year wasn't a good one—it was during exam week, it was cold, the guys who took me around had to take me all the way over to Duke to party—I just got plain homesick.

For a while I went back and forth in my thinking between Richmond and North Carolina and I chose the Tar Heels in the end because people like Mansfield made North Carolina seem like the place for me.

So did my pop. My mom was always the one who gave me most advice, but when my pop had an opinion, I listened. I knew he was very proud that North Carolina, a good football school, had made me an offer—and he never let me forget what an opportunity that represented. I knew he was right—and deep down, homesickness or not, that was what I wanted all along.

When I think back on it now, my senior year in high school was one of those special years when luck or the Lord or some beneficial force out there seemed to be on my side. I came to football late but, it seems, at just the right time.

It was also in my senior year that I formed the closest, most important friendships of my life. When I was younger, I knew some of these guys, but we had never all hung out together. In my senior year, our schedules put us in a lot of the same classes. Because of that, we started hanging out as a group. Till then, I spent most of my time with other football players—but once these old friends of mine and I could move as a group, all that changed.

We did everything together. We drank, we went out on quadruple dates together, we harmonized—and mostly we played cards. It doesn't sound like much. But I tell you, when people asked, "Where are your children?" our folks really could say, "Playing cards!"

We played a game called spades—something like hearts but where you play partners and use spades as trumps along with two jokers and a deuce as high trumps. Sure, we raised hell—mostly with cars. One friend had a light blue Maverick with fifteen-inch Keystone rims. It was like a car my family had, except that our Maverick had Cragars instead of Keystones. I'd "borrow" my parents' cars in the middle of the night and we'd race each other out on Pebblestone Highway or play tag or go on out to the Mooretown Bridge with a case of beer. The main thing between us wasn't hell-raising—or cards. It was a sense that all of us shared about doing our own thing in life—and getting somewhere with it.

In school, people would see one of us and ask, "Where are the rest of you guys?" We had a standard answer: "You've seen one, you've seen us all." We formed a singing group that year called D'Fellas, and we entered ourselves in the school Gong Show. We came in third—and we've been D'Fellas ever since.

When I was rehabilitating myself a year ago, of course I found my way to D'Fellas. How could it be otherwise? They never judged me; they accepted me because they knew who I was when most other people didn't. They didn't need to lecture me or correct me. They got together on their own when they knew I was in trouble and they decided among themselves that one of them would say something to me along the way.

One of them said, "Taylor, our thing isn't drugs." That was all. The rest of it was cards and cars and beer and harmonizing.

They are all such different individuals. None of them

are athletes, none of them are big shots, and not one of them treats me any differently today than when they first met me. I'm not LT to them, just "Taylor."

Dylan Pritchett is the Fella I've known the longest. When I was in second grade, I used to be looked after by a lady called Miss Harris. She lived out in Mooretown. Before she got killed by a hit-and-run driver and I was moved to another baby-sitter, I used to play out there with Pritchett. He lived two doors away and I'd sneak over there—we'd play basketball or go out to Mooretown Bridge. Today Pritchett is the director of black programs at Colonial Williamsburg.

I met John Morning in the fourth grade. John had an Afro out to here and eyeglasses thick as Coke bottles, and he used to go with this real pretty white girl named Trish. I could never take my eyes off this girl. I mean, she was the prettiest girl in school, and here comes this dude from New Jersey—he comes waltzing into the lunchroom one day and this girl suddenly gets up and hollers, "John, oh, Johhnn!" And he's carrying on so cool and looking so weird, I told myself, "I have to get to know this guy. He will lead me to paradise."

J.D. is the lover—and the businessman—in our group. He manages a restaurant chain today.

I got to know Eric Pruden in Sunday school. I became friendly with him because he had the finest sister in two states. I mean, she wasn't pretty, she was beautiful. Aside from my wife, Linda, she was the only other girl I've ever really been in love with. I got close to Eric so I could see her—but when it didn't work out with Darlene, Eric and I remained friends.

He works hard, he has two jobs to keep going. But his thing is reading. He was book smart even as a kid and still is. He reads everything from the back of cereal boxes to books whose names you can't pronounce.

I met Eric Stone—the youngest, by four years, of D'Fellas—because Eric Pruden beat him up one day on the school bus. We just became friends after that—I don't really know why. Eric's a fireman, a hell-raiser, knows everyone in Williamsburg, and will probably be elected mayor of the Burg before his days are done.

Glenn Carter ("Cosmo") was around through junior high but not high school. He linked up with us later—while I was in college—but he and Stoney are the two cornerstones that keep us strong today.

We had such a good time together—there are so many memories. There are the guys jumping out of the stands, running stride for stride with me down the sidelines as I'm on my way to the end zone at Cooley Field!

Here we are on a quadruple date. Two couples in one car, two in the other. Eric Pruden, driving his full-barreled G.T.O., the Blue Ghost, had a yard of space between himself and his date after we parked. It took an hour, but he finally made a move and then suddenly let out this bloodcurdling scream—he jumped out of the car and started running up and down the street, yelling, "The cramps! The cramps!" It wasn't his date, it was just that he was prone to cramps—and forgot his cramp pills that night. We had to hold him down on the pavement to get the cramps out of him.

Now it's our last day at Lafayette High. First period. Pritchett and I decided this was a day for beer, and as we were on good terms with our second-period teacher, we told him what we wanted to do, he excused us, we went and got ripped, and we got back to school later in the morning—just in time to hear an announcement over the loudspeaker:

"Would Dylan Pritchett and Lawrence Taylor please report to the principal's office immediately."

We both thought we had had it.

When we sat down in the guy's office, we were so drunk we could barely see, and both of us were sure the principal could see—and smell—perfectly.

Instead, the principal told us there had been a rumor

circulating that there was going to be a race riot in school that day. As Pritchett was the school president and as I was a respected senior athlete, would we be willing to help cool things out? Oh, yes, we'd be more than willing—it seemed like the least we could do under the circumstances. We were both off the hook.

I was specifically told to make sure the hallways were clear. Think of those words—"keep the hallways clear." Then think of the state I was in. Bell rings. Students start to change classes. They're in the hallways. Can you guess the rest?

Before I could finish cleaning up the hallways—I had hung a lot of people in these wall lockers and closed the doors on them—I was restrained and led back to the principal's office. By then it was clear that Pritchett and I were not quite in our right minds, but because it was Williamsburg and because the principal and school authorities knew us and our families very well, no one thought of damaging our school careers or pressing charges against us.

Pritchett, who is our "philosopher" and who can give you not one but six different explanations for why the world is flat, says that to understand us you really have to understand this town we come from, where everybody knows everybody, where you can be forgiven for being who you are but not for pretending to be someone you are not.

After my troubles a year ago, reporters came down to Williamsburg looking for stories about the guys and me because they thought it might help explain something. A lot of the stories portray us as being small-town, beer-drinking good ole boys who can't quite figure out how to deal with adult life or maybe, even, white life.

Pritchett says that what these stories do is turn D'Fellas into "The Fellas." For me, these guys are my family. I know myself better through them—just as I do through my parents and my school and my town.

I know where I come from. Not all the awards and all the

troubles in the world can change that. The cliché is that when you're a black kid from nowhere all you ever do is overcome poverty. Bull.

One day I was ready to leave this town and these people and go off into the world. Not a weekend in Pittsburgh but years and a career in big cities and big stadiums.

I remember that last day before I left for Chapel Hill. I was in my room packing. My boys were there. We were bullshitting and singing and horsing around. My mom came into the room. She leaned against a dresser with a smile on her face, proud to see her son go off to college.

"Lonnie," she said, "I've got to tell you something."

"What's that, Mama?"

She proceeded to strip my skin away. Everything I ever thought I had gotten away with—from the time I wrecked my pop's truck to cleaning out the hallways at Lafayette High—she gave back to me in the smallest detail.

"But how did you know?"

She was laughing all the while. "Oh, honey," she said, "in this town for every five things you can do there are ten people who know and nine of those people talk to your mama!"

My boys were laughing their asses off.

"Great," I said, "that's great."

She really wasn't trying to put me down or preach to me. She was just having a good time. But I've always remembered that day because it's always reminded me that I could never really travel that far from home and these people I loved.

Around them, I could never be anyone other than myself.

5

WHEN it came time to drive from Williamsburg to North Carolina, I had a hard time keeping my folks from seeing that there was a part of me—a big part of me—that wanted out of this adventure. It was August and it was hot as hell and in a little while my folks were gonna leave me hundreds of miles from home. Chapel Hill, not exactly a metropolis, seemed like one of the population centers of the world. My mom asked me before I unpacked: "Are you sure you want to do this?"

I told her I wasn't sure at all.

My friends might not believe that one because before my days at Carolina were done, I picked up quite a reputation. I was told one day before I cleared out four years later that some folks had taken out a contract on me because they wanted me out of town badly—and, to tell the truth, I can understand.

My first nickname at Carolina was "The Monster." Before the end of my senior year, a lot of folks called me "Filthy McNasty." You might even call my Carolina years "The Saga of Filthy McNasty" and you wouldn't be too far off. If somebody yelled across campus at me, "Heyy, Fiiillltthhhy!" I'd turn around and shout back, "Awwwwrighhht!"

But in the beginning I was no monster. Lafayette had thirty-three, thirty-five guys on the football team. Carolina had over a hundred players and eight or nine coaches. Where I played both ways at Lafayette, here I was lucky to be playing at all. You learned a specialty in college and you stayed with it. At first the coaches weren't even sure whether I'd be an offensive or a defensive player. One coach, Al Grove, fought for me to be a defensive player, thought I would eventually be an outside linebacker—and he won the day. Luck again. He and Jim Tressler, another Carolina staff guy, were the two best position coaches I've ever had—including the Giants.

When I came out for my first practice, the sight of those Carolina players was just plain intimidating. I was 6-1, about 205 pounds—and I was small! Billy Johnson, our fullback, was 265 pounds. Dee Hardison, one of the first people I met, was 280 or 290. The outside linebackers on the team, Kenny Sheets and T. K. McDaniels, were both around 6-6 and 230 pounds.

I couldn't believe I was going to make it there. I kept telling myself, "Who are you fooling? You think you're a football player?" I called my mom almost every night. Somewhere around the third or fourth day of practice we were all in the locker room and suddenly the upperclassmen on the team came in and started pounding on the lockers.

"Freshman day! Freshman day! Freshman day!" They kept shouting. One of them plugged a pair of electric shears into the wall. They grabbed the first freshman they saw and cut a strip right down the center of his skull. The freshman player had a choice. He could walk around like that, or he could have the rest of his hair taken off, too. He didn't dare raise a fuss. And neither did anyone else. When they got to me, I didn't want them to touch me. I had a big, beautiful Afro, and zap, just like that, there was a four-lane highway of skin right through it. But I didn't say a word. I let them do it and then I let them shave me bald.

There were fortunately two weeks to go before students had to show up for the fall semester—and by then I realized that walking around with a bald head was a kind of badge of Carolina football. You got singled out as a Carolina player, and football was very popular on campus.

For those first August days, I had a roommate named Casey. I don't remember much about him because he moved on pretty quickly. He was married, and I guess that was memorable. He was the first married football player I had met in my life! He was also studying for the Christian ministry. He was all right, but I somehow knew we weren't cut out for each other.

My next roommate, the first real roommate I had at Carolina, was a tennis player named Junee Chapman. Junee was a really good guy, a break for me from that early routine of eating, practicing, and sleeping in the summer heat. I mean, I had gotten to the point where all of life consisted of a jockstrap, a pair of shorts, and a shirt. I knew there was more to life—and college—than that. Junee was already part of the Carolina scene, and he didn't seem to have any of the homesick blues I did. He introduced me to a few girls—which was just fine—but then a few weeks later, he had his girlfriend over. No problem there. She spent the night, of course, and I went out to the lounge and slept on the sofa. I was a good roommate. But the next night his girlfriend showed up again and the night after that, too. She just moved right in and I found myself taking up permanent residence in the lounge. The guys on the floor let me hear about it. They'd come in there, see me stretched out on the couch, and they'd say, "Hey, man, is this your room?" "No," I said, and one day I went back inside—where the three of us lived.

That was tough. Junee and his girlfriend weren't in the least bothered by my being there. They'd get into doing their thing, making more noise than you ever heard in your life, and I'd pull a pillow over my head—which only made matters worse. They'd laugh their asses off. The tighter I pulled the pillow over my head, the more they laughed. I couldn't figure out what was so funny. All I wanted to do was go to sleep.

I worked hard on the football field. I did all my drills, all my running, everything as fully as possible. I didn't talk much to the upperclassmen because you didn't do that at Carolina. In fact I stayed quiet, period.

We had three and then two practices a day. On top of that we had meetings, films, study halls, and all the rest. It was a lot compared to Lafayette and *nothing* compared to the Giants. When we reached the end of the day, or when we had to turn our attention to the rest of school, we were just worn out. I remember in that first year, when Bill Dooley was still coach, if we missed one of those two-hour study halls they held for the football team, he'd get your ass out running at six o'clock the next morning. It was called "the sunrise run." The guys who missed study hall the night before would gather in front of the dorm before six and then some assistant coach would drive up and we'd have to run behind him from the dorm to wherever he felt like driving. We wouldn't know where, but somewhere along the line—miles away—he'd wave to us real sweetly and take off.

The most important thing for me in those early days was just to fit in. I sure didn't feel at home right away—either on or off the football field—and the biggest thing for me was doing what I had to do to gain respect.

Now, when I got to Carolina, the football team was loaded with crazies. I mean, serious certifiable crazies, and particularly when it came to the linebacker corps. I learned later on that most linebackers—at least the good ones—have this quality. It seems to go with the territory. The Giants' linebackers certainly have been that way along with most of the good ones around the NFL. I'm not sure why exactly. It may have to do with the position we occupy on the field, halfway between the trenches and the open spaces—you know, halfway betwen reality and fantasy or something. It is an area that demands alertness, improvisation, speed, and a willingness to go all out instantly regardless of the consequences.

At any rate, before I got to Carolina, they had an outside linebacker named Bill Purdue. This guy set a standard for insanity and destruction that people still talk about down there today. There are plenty of people who will tell you they were with Bill Purdue when he started smashing bottles in a bar—so he could eat the glass. One of Bill Purdue's "things" was to eat glass. Or so the legend goes.

Another was to smash things up. There's a Bill Purdue story about kicking in a dormitory door at three o'clock in the morning and simply taking a room and its inhabitants apart—just for the hell of it. There's a Bill Purdue story for just about every piece of mayhem known to man.

When I arrived on the scene, Bill Purdue was gone, though his reputation lingered. There were other players on the team, other linebackers, who were full-fledged crazies on their own. This was a Carolina football tradition. Buddy Curry, who now plays for the Atlanta Falcons, and Donnell Thompson, currently on the Colts, were a match for anyone. There was another pair of linebackers, Ron Wooten, who plays for the Patriots, and Rick Donnelly, who went on to play for the Redskins, who even went beyond crazy— they were just sick. These two were chemistry majors—and smart (that is, in terms of learning what was in chemistry books). One day, after two other players pulled some sort of practical joke on them, they brought a test tube full of magic back from their lab and poured it under the door where these guys roomed. Within ten seconds the rooms were on fire.

Now, anybody who came into the Carolina football program knew all about the craziness that went with it. If you were a freshman there were certain bars off Franklin Street that you just did not dare walk into because if you did, upperclassmen on the team would beat your ass within an inch of your life.

The dormitory—Ehring House—where we all lived was like a scene out of *Animal House*. Something like the delivery of pizza to the dorm would turn the whole place upside down, with guys throwing things—including heavy pieces of furniture—down stairwells and out windows. One guy who had missed spring practice and then an entire season because he had torn up both his shoulders heaved a big desk out the window one night—I guess proving that his shoulders were okay—and got himself promptly thrown out of school.

I think this craziness wouldn't even be worth mentioning but for football. The only place where respect counted on the Carolina football team was—naturally—on the football field. If you had lived in Ehring House when I did, you would have seen something on game day. Early in the morning, eight o'clock or so, guys would move their stereos out onto the balconies and let them rip. The music would be blasting and everyone would be standing around bullshitting and knocking down the fuel till five minutes before we had to go to the stadium. Then, believe me, it was all business. You never saw such a transformation in your life. In my freshman year, when this team showed up, it always showed up ready to do serious damage. These guys all knew by heart where all that madness was supposed to go.

I didn't. Oh, I knew from the beginning that whatever I did had to come out on the football field first. And I know for sure that a lot of the style I later brought to the pros, of all-out play with a kind of reckless abandon, came right out of my Carolina days when I began to understand craziness wasn't just for asylums.

But at first I didn't know where I fit in as a football player. I was on special teams in my freshman year. For a while I didn't even know if I'd make the team. It was a big thrill for me when the names of the traveling squad—the varsity—were posted and my name was included. I half expected to be sent off to the freshman team, but I never was.

I didn't play much. I spent a lot of time on the bench paying special attention to Kenny Sheets, one of our all-ACC linebackers. I think I learned a lot from just watching his moves. He wasn't especially fast, but he did some things you would not believe. He played the run better than anyone. He knew how to play all the blocks. That freshman year I didn't even want to get into the games, I was content to play special teams. Anything else would have been too hard mentally—I wasn't yet ready for college football. But that didn't stop me at all. If I couldn't play much, I still could do things on a football field to gain the respect of my teammates.

I used to rush downfield as though nothing could stand in my way. When I was going for the ballcarrier, I would go through, under, and around—and over—anyone. I made it a special point to dive over blocking players to get at a ballcarrier. If there was a fullback in front of me, I'd go right up over him. I'd get flipped on my ass just about every time, but I didn't care. I'd go right after them the next time—even though the chances were nine in ten that I would get turned upside down and sent to the ground like a plane crash.

Sometimes I'd make it through. I'd get to the ballcarrier and I'd club him down, then leap up and scream! My teammates used to love that and so did the fans. The more they let me know, the more I did it. It got to be a signature of mine. "The Monster Cry," they called it. I'd hit a guy, leap up, throw my head back, and let go with that huge old monster cry! Whatever anyone else thought, I loved it, too.

But I was never sure in those days that I could fit in as a football player, that anyone would really come to respect me for the player I was—or might be. Respect was everything. The one area where I could prove myself as a Carolina crazy was *off* the field. There I could be a match for anyone, and I told myself early on that I would be the craziest of the crazies, the wildest one of all.

I went into bars and pool halls looking for fights—and I nearly always found them. One night I was in a place having a real good run at nine-ball—I made a lot of extra money at nine-ball during my Carolina years. Finally one guy beat me. When the game was over, he took this glass of beer and slammed it on the table, sending it all over me.

"Why'd you do that?" I asked.

"Because I felt like it," he said. The guy strutted over to rack up the balls for the next game. I walked up to him, took my glass of beer, and poured it down his neck. The guy jumped up and screamed.

"Why did you do that?"

"Because I felt like it," I said.

He took a swing at me. The rest was Wild West. I don't know how much damage was done to this place, but it was considerable.

In the bars behind Franklin Street, I raised all kinds of hell. One night, we parked ourselves in Mayo's, way in the back near the storage cooler and, because we were broke and drunk and having a good time, lifted seven or eight cases of Heineken from the cooler. We drank to our heart's content and in the meantime gave beers away to everyone in sight. We sold some, too, because we were so low on funds. The crowds in Mayo's were so thick nobody knew a thing—except those who were getting drunk with us.

I didn't have a secure position on the team, but I was getting one down behind Franklin Street. I was determined to leave Bill Purdue in the dust.

One night I was standing around at a bar with a bunch of guys, a number of basketball players—Mike O'Koren, Phil Ford, Al Wood, Walter Davis—and some football players. Everyone was into acting real tough. I don't know what it is about a bunch of guys all of whom consider themselves top guns, but they have a way of turning any place into Dodge City. They were loud and laughing and having a hell of a time and I remember one of them took a glass, drank down his beer, and then made a point of just breaking the glass. All the guys got off on that. What I did was to then take another glass, break it on the side of the bar and then begin eating it.

I watched the faces of these guys go red. They couldn't believe what they were seeing. You can swallow that stuff, too—I did. You can't digest it, of course, but you can get it from one pipe to the other. It wasn't sane, it was hell on my mouth, but I survived all right—and those guys never looked at me quite the same way again.

One night I came home with a bunch of guys, and instead of going in the front door of Ehring House with them, I told them I was going to go up to my room on the sixth floor another way. I had noticed that the brickwork on the front of the building had these little ridges in it and I had wondered for a while if it was possible to climb the face of the building that way. I tried and made it—the way these professional lunatics with suction cups do it, only without the suction cups. Then I got to doing it regularly. Guys would watch me, baffled and amazed—and then they would goad me to it. And I would oblige—day or night. I did it even when I was blind drunk. When I was that far out of it I never had to think about what might happen if I slipped or why I ever did this in the first place. Brick by brick I climbed my way—except that it wasn't on a football field, the only place where it really counted.

The funny part is that if you want to understand what you see out there on Sunday afternoons going after NFL quarterbacks, you better understand this monster on the bricks. Back then, when I didn't really know who I was or where I was going, I had this feeling that nothing was going to shut me out—same as I do today when I'm lined up with smoke coming out of my ears, waiting to go. In Chapel Hill, I started out as one anonymous person among thousands of others. Nobody knew me then on a football field. You earned respect by finding the biggest guy you could find and knocking him on his ass. They learned your name pretty fast when they saw you go six stories up the face of a building in the middle of the night, blind drunk.

WE had a new head coach, Dick Crum, beginning in my sophomore season. For me and most of the guys, the change was anything but welcome. Bill Dooley, the head coach at Carolina when I arrived there, had definitely been successful. He had just come off a year where he had won an ACC championship, and his departure was a move up for him. He got a job as athletic director as well as head football coach at Virginia Tech. But it was a move down for Carolina football.

Dools had always been a players' coach. He knew what a big-time college football team was, and he didn't bullshit you about being scholar-athletes and responsible citizens. He was into winning—and into looking after his players. Without any of the pious bullshit you get from other folks, Dools respected the people he dealt with. His coaches were all first-rate people, and they were allowed as much latitude as they needed to mold a winning football team. You didn't see Dools too much, you rarely wound up talking to the guy because he delegated responsibility to everyone else. The defensive coordinator really took care of the defense, the offensive guys really took care of the offense.

Dools wasn't into turning the system on its head, but he made sure players weren't going to get too hassled with their courses or with the university administration. He knew a

Getting together with Ron Jaworski—action just the way I love it. Will he remember? I hope so. I want quarterbacks to think about me all the time. *Photo © Fred Roe*

My folks. They worked all the time when I was a kid and there wasn't much time for picture-taking—but here's a shot I've kept with me. Here are my father, mother, grandmother, along with my brothers and me (Kim is left; Buddy, right).

The Taylor gang: Kim (*left*), Buddy (*right*), and me. We look sweet here, but my mother says that the three of us —at this age—once jumped a cop and took his gun.

I went from nobody of the year to Male Athlete of the Year in my senior year at Lafayette High. Here I am with another "Senior Superlative"—her name escapes me but she was Female Athlete of the Year.

Pete Babcock "discovered" me for the Williamsburg Jaycees, my first football team. My real motivation in playing for the Jaycees was not football, but a trip to Pittsburgh—as far from home as I'd ever been. *Photo by David Falkner*

Coach Melvin Jones of Lafayette High, builder of dreams and football teams. He has a saying for every occasion—as you can see from all the writing on the wall. Without Coach Jones, I don't know if I ever would have had a football career. *Photo by David Falkner*

Starting from the left, that's Dylan Pritchett, Eric Pruden, me, Eric Stone, John Morning (J.D.) and Paul Davis. Except for Paul, whom I met at Chapel Hill, we've all been hanging out together since childhood—so long, in fact, that we just call ourselves D'Fellas. None of these guys are athletes, all of them are my closest friends. *Photo © Chris Schwenk*

No discussion or photo of D'Fellas would be complete, of course, without mentioning Glen Carter (Cosmo), at right. He's a cornerstone of the group, but somehow he missed the gathering above. *Photo by David Falkner*

Steve Streater as a
Carolina football player.
He was my roommate and
closest friend for three
years in Chapel Hill. He
was paralyzed after a car
crash at the time of the
pro football draft in 1981.
I dedicated my rookie
season to Steve. *UNC
Publicity*

My friend and agent Ivery
Black. Ivery helped get
me to the pros—and to
stay there when I crashed
a year ago.

You can't tell I was a wild man at Carolina from this picture—or can you? There were folks who wanted me out of Chapel Hill badly enough, I was told, to put a contract out on me. *UNC Publicity*

Linda and I met at Chapel Hill and got married after my first year in the pros. We sat for a 1986 Christmas card with our children, T.J., Tenitia, and Paula. Paul Davis is standing next to me. *Photo © Chris Schwenk*

Here I am at practice before my rookie year (Number 98 never suited me). *Photo © Fred Roe*

Here I am in my first season, recovering a Tony Dorsett fumble in a 13–10 win over Dallas that got us into the playoffs. *AP/Wide World Photos*

1981 turned out to be a great year. I was both Rookie of the Year and Defensive Player of the Year. *Photo © Fred Roe*

team was really made up of a lot of people who had to live together and jell together in their work. He made you get out in the damn predawn if you cut a study hall, and he used to run a curfew on us before games, but, well, that was something different.

He'd drive his car up into the lot outside Ehring House right around the time for lights out and wait until he saw the place go dark. The football players were all in one wing of the dormitory, so it was easy to keep tabs on us. It was also easy for us to keep tabs on him. As soon as his car nosed out of the parking lot and turned a corner, all the lights snapped on, seemingly at once. The stereos would be blasting, the showers running, the hair driers blowing in the wind. There was a heavy night of partying ahead—a lot to pack in before kickoff. As long as we kept our part of the bargain on Saturday afternoons—which we did—everything was fine.

He made sure we ate together, slept together, talked football together—and partied together. On Friday nights we all went to the movies together, the whole Carolina team. We used to have a team meeting and vote on what picture we were going to go to, and then Dools would rent out the theater for us and off we'd go.

We were able to fool Dools into looking after us in little ways coaches get blasted for. If you needed extra tickets for the game—that is, extra spending money, because selling game tickets is one of the standard ways football players have of getting by—we'd come up with this or that valid excuse and he'd provide. Ditto with basketball tickets or the use of field-house cars—we had recruits to look after, to show around.

It was a joy to play for Dools. He never forgot that the game of football, whatever else it was, was also fun. The meetings his coaches held, particularly those of Coach John Harper, were funny and lively—as well as important in our preparation. And though Dools hung back and let others take the credit and do the talking, every once in a while he'd make an appearance. Not these Knute Rockne-type locker-room appearances, but the kind that showed you he was aware that his football players were human beings.

I think the only conversation I ever had with him was when he showed up unannounced at the dorm one night. He wasn't checking up on anyone, he was just letting us know that even if we didn't see much of him, he was with us. He came to my room and spent some time with me. I happened to have my walls plastered with pictures I had drawn—among them, several of Coach Dooley.

He looked at these pictures, turned to me, and said, "These are really good. I never knew you could do that."

I felt so flattered, it was like he had complimented me about my playing. I started drawing like crazy after that. Actually, I had always liked drawing. I had been fooling around since the third grade—had a girlfriend then who taught me a few techniques. I also had a cousin who happened to be a first-rate artist, and he spent quite a bit of time showing me things about drawing.

Anyway, Dools was pleased that I had drawn a good likeness of him, and though I wouldn't have made a point of showing him my work, I took his interest in my drawing as an interest in me, one of the football players who played for him.

Dick Crum was totally different. As much fun as there had been playing under Dools, there was the lack of it playing for Crum. He brought in his own staff of people with him, and he treated them like errand boys. He wanted to do everything himself. His coaches—save for one, whom he eventually fired—were terrified of him and never had the balls to call him on anything.

Crum knew the game of football all right, but he had never played it and never bothered to learn that human beings—not Xs and Os on a chalkboard—were the ones who went out there to make things happen.

He set out to undo everything Coach Dooley left behind.

The idea that players should live together, apart from the rest of the college community, bothered him. He split us all up, so that it took till late in the season even to learn the names of the guys you played next to on the field. Sometimes you wouldn't see other guys from the team at all unless it was at practice or at the games.

Maybe Crum thought he was improving our lives or something, but football is a team sport. In order to play really well on a high level you *have* to be like a family, even if you aren't. The closer you get, the better your chances of success. If you know somebody's problems, you start to know how to help him. A guy who is with you so much he knows which way you're going to move in the dark will also know what you're going to do when a play is run around your end. It's not a matter of getting off on your teammates, it's a matter of collective power, which is what the game of football is all about. Even guys who don't play, who are on the bench or down with injuries can be a part of it. Take the Giants this past season. We won because we had that kind of togetherness. You saw it on the field, we had it off the field. A guy like Curtis McGriff—the seventh-year defensive end from Alabama—who had been out the whole year with a knee injury was as important as anyone else. Ole Curtis! Damn. Curtis's father was supposed to have been one of the greatest storytellers in the state of Alabama. Well, Curtis has always tried to follow in his father's footsteps. The only thing is his deep Alabama drawl makes almost everything he says completely incomprehensible. It doesn't matter. He kept us howling with his stories anyway.

Every winning team needs a Curtis McGriff.

Crum looked at his players like they were so many cases for rehab and correction. One of the first team meetings we had, a guy walked into the session ten seconds late—ten seconds—and Crum threw him out of the room. We had scores of players who chewed tobacco. Under Coach Dooley we sat in meetings with our cups and nobody ever said anything.

Bad habit, no doubt, but nobody ever was so paranoid they took it as some sort of personal insult—until Dick Crum. The first time Dick saw us in there with our wads and cups, he didn't just make us get rid of them, he made us swallow the loads in our mouths! He endeared himself to us with that.

We went from being ACC champs to being 5–6 in Crum's first year, in spite of the fact that pretty nearly everybody from our championship team had returned. A month into Crum's regime, there were no cars, no extra tickets, no living together, no movies on Friday nights, no looking the other way over partying. The night before a game, Crum moved us into a hotel. If we wanted to watch movies, he said, we could tune in our TVs.

I don't mind saying there was never any love lost between Dick Crum and myself. I heard second and third hand that when I was drafted, Crum was up there telling people not to take me because I was "uncoachable" and undisciplined. I have no idea if that ever happened, but if it did, I wouldn't be surprised. That was Crum's style.

My linebacker coach, Jim Tressler, was the one person on Crum's staff who had a mind of his own. He went out of his way to help me, and he stood up to Dick Crum when he had to. One time, during the season, Crum got all over me for not doing something he thought I should have done. Crum started yelling at me in the locker room, and Jim came over and said, "Don't jump on him, jump on me. I told him to run the play he did."

Crum couldn't stand the idea of one of his coaches challenging him. He flipped out. "If you want a piece of me, why don't we go outside and settle it now!" Real bright.

Tressler wasn't scared of Crum in the least. He stood there toe to toe with him, arguing. If Crum had thrown a punch, Tressler would have come right back at him. Crum didn't throw a punch. He just fired him. Not then. Later, after we upset Michigan in the Gator Bowl. The man was devastated. Crum fired him for God knows what reason, but what I know was that Jim, from day one, refused to kiss his ass. That was a fatal mistake in the Gospel According to Crum.

Anyway, I wound up starting in my sophomore year as an inside linebacker, alongside Buddy Curry. On the first play of the second quarter of the first game of the year, I cracked a bone in my foot, and that was the extent of my being a starter for a while. When I got back into action several weeks later, Darryl Nicholson had taken my linebacker job and was playing really well. I was moved all over the field. I played nose guard for a while—hated it—and then, in one game against North Carolina State, I wound up playing nose tackle, inside linebacker, and outside linebacker on different shifts. I left the field that day in a daze. Halfway through my sophomore year, I had become convinced there was absolutely no chance I would ever play pro ball. I also remember wanting, very badly, to simply quit the football team. It was only because quitting meant having to leave school that I stayed on. If I left school, I didn't know what I might wind up doing. There was no way I wanted to face that.

At the end of that season I decided on something else, along with six other players on the Carolina team. Donnell Thompson, Steve Streater, Tyrus Bratton, Harry Stainback, and I—and maybe a couple of other guys—decided we would all transfer together to the University of Kansas. One of the guys had looked into it, we found it was quite doable, and we would have gone ahead but for the fact that some really powerful alumni had gotten wind of this and stepped in in time to talk us out of it.

Meanwhile, life just seemed to get crazier and crazier at Carolina. Who knew where that was heading? From the second half of my freshman year right through the end of my first semester as a senior, I roomed with Steve Streater. I could count on him for anything—and he could count on me. A lot of times, we'd just do things like play basketball. We got into these pickup games—real serious ones—with guys like James Worthy, Michael Jordan, Al Wood, and so on. We did all right. Steve was small, but he scored like crazy. I was 6-3—but I could jump through the gym, played very physically, and had a jump shot from thirty feet. Michael once told a reporter from *USA Today* that I was the toughest of all the Carolina basketball players he had ever come up against. I don't know about that. I played him—like he played me—pretty hard. But I sure was no better than anyone else at holding him down. When Michael Jordan gets that funny little look in his eye and his tongue comes slithering out between his teeth, forget it—you and the whole NBA are dead.

But Steve and I were into far crazier sports than basketball. Very often we'd go into Steve's suite—he had a roommate who wasn't around on the weekends. But now on Friday nights sometimes, Steve and I would sit around when this other roommate wasn't there and we'd turn off the lights, put on Earth, Wind, and Fire, get wrecked, then head on uptown and go nuts.

One night we were rolling out of one bar on our way to another and some dude starts leaning on Steve out in the street. Now, Steve really was no bigger than 5-7 or 5-8, and this guy who got on him was as big and nasty as could be.

"Don't fuck with me, I got a gun!" He shouted at Steve. This wasn't your typical college invitation to the dance, but Steve didn't bat an eye. He just stood there, squinting like Clint Eastwood.

All our friends suddenly scrambled and got the hell out of the way. I didn't know what was going to happen, but I sure wasn't going to leave Steve there to find out alone.

"I got a gun right here and I'm gonna use it!" the guy shouted. He was tapping this bulge in his back pocket. He *looked* as crazy as we actually were.

"I got a fucking gun, too," I screamed back. "Why don't you use yours?"

The guy stopped dead in his tracks. He didn't know what to make of that. Steve and I both began to play with our back pockets like we were carrying pieces. The guy finally cursed and walked off. I wonder what was in *his* back pocket?

Craziness, stupidity, recklessness—and loyalty: They all went together in Carolina. The only problem was that the further I got away from making it as a football player, the more out of control I seemed to get. I reached a point where I could no longer separate in my mind the difference between having someone fear you and respect you. Midway through my sophomore year, I was a regular visitor to the police station. I don't know how many times I had been taken down there to "cool off." In my enlightened state, I never regarded the cops as anything more than harmless flies. The F Troop, I called them—after the TV sitcom.

One time, Steve and Paul Davis and a few other friends saved my ass from the police. It was snowing that night, one of the few times it ever snowed in Chapel Hill. The sight of snow in Chapel Hill was enough to put everybody on tilt. Franklin Street turned into *Star Wars* with snowballs.

The guys and I had come rolling out of the last bar of the night on our way home, and sure enough, we got into this snowball fiesta with everyone else. Only we were really out of it—and I was beyond that, veering toward some black hole. These cars would come to a stop at this red light and we would just let them have it—like everyone else. But this one guy in a jeep got pissed off and started jawing at us. That was enough for me.

I went around to the back of his jeep—it had this big square canvas covering with a large plastic window in the rear. I took a running jump and dove straight through, crashing into the front seat next to the driver. I grabbed ahold of him, had an armlock around his neck, and the guy was screaming. I thought he was going to have a heart attack. As soon as I jumped out of the jeep, he took off at zero max. Fun, huh? That was only the curtain raiser.

A cop—a city cop, I think—saw all this from a block away and came cruising up to us. He stopped, got out, and came on over.

"Which one of you wants to pay for a broken window?" he said.

I stepped right out in front.

"How much does it cost?"

"How much have you got?" the cop said.

"About thirty-seven cents," I said.

"You want to get smart?" he asked.

"I'll get any way I want," I said. I didn't give a shit. The cop pulls out his nightstick. I said: "What are you gonna do with that?"

"I'm going to use it if I have to," he said.

"You use that thing," I said, enjoying myself hugely, "I'll wrap it around your motherfucking head."

London School of Diplomacy, no, but what the hell, I figured it was the F Troop, and I surely was feeling no pain. The next thing I knew—I guess the guy must have hit his car radio while I was standing there admiring myself—the place was suddenly swarming with cop cars, all of them with their party hats flashing. We were all surrounded, but it was me they had in mind.

"Where is your ID?" they wanted to know. I still wasn't impressed.

"I tell you what," I said. "I'm not showing you ID because I don't have ID."

They started talking about taking some of us down to the station house. That also didn't seem like much of a threat.

"I'm not going anywhere," I said, feeling just as pleased as I could be. Little did I know that was the straw that broke the camel's back. In a flash, the whole bunch of them were on top of me. I swear, in two seconds I was spread-eagled across a car, my hands twisted behind me, cuffs cutting into my wrists. I was pinned there, beer bottles hanging out of my pockets, my breath likely to blow any Breathalyzer machine off the charts, and these dudes in a red-ass fury.

The guys saved me from myself—and from the troop. Buddy Curry and Paul Davis and a couple of other guys came over and pleaded with the cops, told them I was a Carolina football player and that I had just plain had one too many. Please, they said, as nice as could be, just let us take the poor sucker home and put him to bed. The cops talked about it for a while and then—I guess because it was true—said okay, take him home.

The cops turned and started to go but as the guys were dragging me off, somehow I felt cheated.

"You sorry sonsuvbitches," I hollered at the cops, "I could've whipped all your asses!"

The guys put heavier hands on me than the cops.

"Shut up, asshole," they kept saying. They dragged me off like I was stolen property.

Looking back on it, I think it's fair to say that halfway through my junior year I was halfway to nowhere. I might not have said so at the time, but I had given up. I had no idea what I'd wind up doing, I didn't even want to think about it. About the only thing left was the ability to be a great troublemaker.

Two things happened—at exactly the same time—to change my life. One Saturday afternoon I played one great football game against North Carolina State. That night I met Linda Cooley—the woman I married. It was like it was meant to be, both things happening like that. Call it luck, call it destiny, whatever you want, but it seemed to be a part of my life that at every critical stage, just when it seemed like I was over the edge, something happened—like it had all been arranged beforehand—to pull me back and turn me around.

7

NORTH CAROLINA State was traditionally our biggest game, and that year was no different. State had a powerful team, had been playing really well when we ran into them in Raleigh the fifth week of the season. The game surged back and forth, had plenty of scoring and big plays, and was in doubt till the very end. We could as easily have lost as won.

Late in the fourth quarter, State began a march on us when we were leading by a touchdown, 28–21. They moved the ball as they had all afternoon, and we just couldn't seem to stop them. They marched down inside our twenty and it seemed inevitable that we were looking at a tie or a one-point State win. The game was in their stadium and the place was going wild. The State quarterback, I forget his name, dropped back to pass on a first- or second-down play. He had beaten us all day and was looking to do it one more time. I didn't have a clear read on this play but instinct told me just to go.

I rushed the way I always did—as though nothing was in my way. State wanted our ass, I wanted State's quarterback. And I got him just as he was going to pass. I hit him like a block of cement falling from a rooftop. The ball popped high out of the guy's grip, he went to the deck with me right on top of him. The referee ruled that the quarterback's arm hadn't come forward—it was a fumble—and we recovered.

There were howls of protest from the State side, but the play stood, and we had possession. We turned around and moved right up the field and down their throats. We scored and put the game away, 35–21.

Because the play I made was both big and controversial, there was a lot of talk about it afterward and for the rest of the season. They kept showing the thing over and over on TV and always with the same look of destruction there regardless of what anyone thought about its being a fumble or not. I looked great, and people began saying all kinds of good things about me as an outside linebacker.

I felt so good afterward, so rewarded by playing well, that I couldn't imagine how anything else could ever have taken the place of doing my best on a football field. Between football and cleaning out a bar or a poolroom, what was the real choice? The will to work hard at something I truly loved and could be good at—or proving to one and all that I was an asshole?

When I went to Mayo's that night, I sure didn't have anything but that old sense of good times burning through me. I could have put away seven cases of this and two bottles of that. But instead I met Linda.

I had seen her around a few times, wondered who she was, then all of a sudden this night we were both standing near each other outside the place. She was near this railing, about to perch herself on it, and about as fast as the thought flashed through my mind that I really would like to check this lady out, I stuck my hand down on the railing so that she would have to sit down at her own peril. We laughed at that. Then we got into a brief conversation and eventually I asked her for her address and phone number. She gave them to me.

I went over to her house the very next day. Her mother

let me in. The house they had was neat, a real family place, and there was Linda sitting in the dining room doing homework. She was dressed in this little hospital-type uniform that made her look just cute as hell. She had a job of some sort and she was going to some community college in Durham. She talked real sweet and simple and she seemed to be about as far from the sort of women I had been hanging around with as could be. I stayed with her for a while and asked her for a regular date—something far from my usual caveman style of one-night stands. I felt so strange. When I got back to the dorm, I told Steve, "I just met the woman I'm going to marry!"

He hadn't thought I was crazy till then.

But when I took up with Linda, I dated her. Just that. We went to Mayo's together, sure—but we didn't hang out. We sat down in a booth. We looked at menus and at each other and we talked. Guys saw us and came over and said, "Taylor, what in hell's the matter with you?"

Linda laughed at that. I did, too—though I also wondered what was wrong with me. I had taken one look at Linda and suddenly I didn't want to go uptown anymore. I had no interest in doing anything crazier than sitting home waiting for the phone to ring. And I did that—for hours, sometimes, so that my friends would just stand there and start teasing me. It didn't change anything. Sometimes if the guys got to me, I'd get pissed off, go uptown, and get in a brawl just to keep my hand in, but I had Linda on my mind, oh, yes!

I didn't know if she cared about me or not. I was too damn proud and too damn scared to tell her what I felt or, sometimes, even to pick up the phone and call her. If she ever said, "I'll call you," I'd just sit there waiting for the phone to ring. I remember there were times when I would pull up a chair next to the telephone, my mind a blank, waiting for the thing to ring. Sometimes hours, evenings went by that way. I didn't care.

I took Linda home with me a couple of months after we had started seeing each other. I say "seeing each other" because I hadn't yet touched her or been able to figure out if she even liked me. She had had a boyfriend recently and this dude used to show up from time to time and I couldn't stand the sight of him. For all I knew—and feared—she cared more about him than me.

Anyway, when we got down to Virginia, we went straight on to Hampton, where Eric Pruden and Dylan Pritchett had rented a house together. Sure, they were glad to see me—I was glad to see them. They knew me without having to guess at anything.

"Hey, man, what'd you bring a woman for? We're all goin' out to line up some trim tonight ourselves!"

I knew they were kidding around. They were laughing and having a fine old time—and the last thing I could do was show them that I wasn't.

"Don't mind her," I said, "she's just along for the ride!"

"No kidding," they said, enjoying the hell out of me.

Linda didn't say anything. She just stopped talking to me altogether. That whole night she stayed real quiet and cold, and the next day when we were at my folks' house she hung around with my mom, talking to her, but not a word to me.

"What the hell's the matter?" I finally said.

"Just along for the ride, huh?" she answered—that was it. No more talk after that. Not then, not on the car ride back to Chapel Hill—not for the next two months. Try as I might, it was like I no longer existed. I'd call her at home: "Sorry, Linda's not here." I'd see her around, she'd pretend I wasn't in the same room. After a while it seemed like it really was over. I had been paid back in full for being the biggest fool in the world.

I had just about gotten over her and started going with this other girl—not someone I really liked but who took up my time—when one night we went to this party. Linda was there with another guy. And during the course of the evening, she just started talking to me. I don't know why, I never bothered to ask—I just stayed with her. And we've been together ever since.

I think the guys were more surprised than I was by the change that came over me, but maybe I was a trend-setter because before long, most of them—Steve Streater, Donnell Thompson, Tyrus Bratton—all got themselves serious girlfriends. We started going to the Saturday-night movies instead of the Saturday-night fights.

Linda had some things to say to me along the way that made me stop and think. She never pushed anything, because I wouldn't have listened—the only person who can change me is me. But why, she wanted to know, was I such a bully? What did I get out of it? I never thought I was a bully, just that I was wild. She just sort of shrugged.

I couldn't really tell her because I hadn't ever really figured it out myself, but I came to see that I had certain priorities mixed up. The big thing for me in Carolina was gaining respect. But I didn't know the difference between fear and respect—which meant that I didn't quite know how to get respect. You beat the shit out of somebody, they'll stay pretty far away from you, they'll even listen when you speak—but the attention you get won't have anything to do with real respect. Respect comes when people not only listen to you but also believe that what you have to say matters—people might not like you, but they'll acknowledge that what you say and do matters.

Respecting yourself is even more important. I got that through football. When I go out on a field, I tell myself I'm the best until someone can prove otherwise. I don't have to bring the fight to anybody, they have to bring it to me. I don't have to play dirty or cheat or brag—I just have to play hard and by the rules—and I don't need anyone to puff up my ego or to try to tear it down, to tell me how good or how bad I am.

It's there in what I do. And what I do is who I am. You look around the league and you'll see players who, through their game, have come to win respect from others and who obviously have real respect for themselves. Walter Payton is like that. People hit him hard and play hard against him all the time, but they'll help him up after they knock him down. Mike Singletary is another example—a very hard-nosed, very intense ballplayer. He never does it dirty, he doesn't ever have to—and he knows that about himself. It's a point of pride with him. He just plays hard, very hard, and he stays within the rules. You watch guys on our own team, guys like Harry Carson and George Martin, guys who have been around for years and have paid their dues. One has been an All-Pro, the other has not; one has been in the limelight, the other has not. Both guys just go out there and do their job with as much intensity as they had when they were rookies—and everybody in the league knows that and respects them for it.

That last year and a half of football at Carolina was everything for me. After that State game in my junior year, I played well every week. I just needed a taste of what playing full tilt and well was all about. The feeling was so damn good, I told myself that if it can be this way one week, why not the following week and the week after that? I didn't need a coach or a preacher to let me know that what I was getting on a football field I could never get in a bar. Linda was important to me and football was important. Simple.

At the end of my junior year, we finished with an 8–3–1 record and went on to the Gator Bowl against Michigan. We were supposed to lose. Instead, we won, 17–15. On one play, I hit their quarterback, John Wangler, and broke his leg. Remembering it now, I can think of it alongside Joe Theismann. But between those two, there was a big, big difference for me. I could walk away from the hit in the Gator Bowl, any injury on a college field, because you wouldn't know the guy you hit and probably wouldn't ever play against him again.

In the pros, the guys you hit are the guys you play against all the time. Now, there are two things about me. One is contact. I love it. It's something you can't really explain, especially when you hit somebody. Normally, you hit them hard and they go straight back—and you feel your body just crunching theirs. But then there's this thing of injuring someone you know, who is a person rather than an anonymous player with a number on his back.

I also happen to hate the sight of blood. There was blood after I hit Joe—this person I knew well enough to know who liked him and who didn't around the league.

I had always heard stories about being able to hear a bone break across the field. I could actually hear Joe's bone breaking. Then I saw his leg, what had happened, saw him rolling and rolling around in agony, and I just knew what he was going through. Another key to my game happens to be this ability to put myself in another player's body, usually to dope out what he's going to do, but this time it worked out so that I was in agony with another player.

The TV cameras caught me clapping my hands against my helmet. But what they didn't pick up was that I was standing on one foot, rubbing it with the other foot. I mean, I was in Joe's body. I can't really explain it. When I watch a movie and see scary situations where people are about to be hurt or even embarrassed, I'll anticipate that in my body. If someone's in real pain, I'll get up and walk out of the room. I couldn't walk out of RFK Stadium, though.

But I could walk away from John Wangler that day because he was just another player I would never see again. Part of the game.

I picked up as a player in my senior year right where I left off in my junior year—only our team, Dools's last freshman class at Carolina, all seniors now, was that much better. We lost only once that year, to Oklahoma, on our way to an

11–1 season and an appearance in the Bluebonnet Bowl. I had another burst of growth between my freshman and sophomore years so that I was full-sized—6-3 and 230—and somehow with size and strength, I had gotten even faster.

In this Bluebonnet Bowl game, we beat Texas 16–7, and the Longhorns had a back named Herky Walls, who had been a sprint champion. On one play he ran a reverse and took off down the sideline with nobody in front of him. I pursued him for sixty yards and got him. In the pros, that's become a calling card of mine—chasing a guy across the field, catching him from behind—and I love it every bit as much as hitting. I don't know how many backs I've done that to, but when I get to them, whether it's a Tony Dorsett or an Eric Dickerson, they'll turn around and give me this look— no words—but their eyes will be saying, "Oh, no, not *you!*"

When I caught Herky Wells, the guy looked at me like he had been caught in a schoolyard with his dick out.

I played for Linda on Saturday afternoons. And I played for myself. People started coming up to me a little differently than they had. They started asking my opinion of this and that. The type of respect I had been looking for all along came from playing good, hard football week after week.

With all of that, the way ahead wasn't on any nice big highway leading straight to the NFL. There were still a few curves in the road, and with the speed I traveled, it took something like luck—once again—to get there in one piece. I mean that quite literally. I'm not making pretty pictures. I came *this* close, it turned out, to getting kicked off the Tar Heels football team, out of the University of North Carolina, and out of any realistic chance to play college football elsewhere—when I needed a big season to go on to the pros.

One day, toward the end of my junior year, Streater and I turned out for a thing called Derby Day at Ehring Field. Once a year all the white frats got together with fifty kegs of beer and ran sack hops and three-legged races, sold food and

T-shirts, and so on. We were walking around out there when all of a sudden Streater hands me this huge stack of T-shirts to hold for him. I didn't know where or how he got them, but it was pretty clear that (1) they hadn't dropped down from heaven and (2) he hadn't paid for them. I held them for him while he went off to go to the bathroom or to make a call or something. The next thing I knew this dude comes up to me and tells me to give him back the shirts. I told him I wouldn't because they weren't mine to give—I was holding them for a friend.

The guy looked a little nutso.

"Give 'em back!" he shouted.

I started to turn away and suddenly he grabs the pile out of my arms and takes off. I ran right after him. When he heard me closing in on him, he suddenly dropped the shirts, turned, and tried to tackle me or throw his arms around me to protect himself, I'm not sure which—but in any case, his instincts were right because I let go this roundhouse punch that would have killed him if it had ever landed. It didn't. Instead, we scuffled around for a bit until this lady wearing a halter and shorts came up to us. Now, I didn't know her from a hole in the wall and so when she started in on me, I just lit into her.

"You bitch, where do you get off saying anything to me when you don't even know what the fuck happened?" Something like that. Accuracy in this case hardly mattered. The lady, it turned out, was the dean of students. I didn't know it till she told me, but even when she did, I let her know that I didn't care if she was the Queen of England. Bright is bright.

The F Troop came around to my rooms that night to investigate—that didn't bother me. But a week later, I got this official-looking letter in the campus mail telling me I had to appear before Honors Court.

I knew about Honors Court because I had once been

threatened with it when I had expropriated some campus furniture for my rooms a couple of years before, but frankly I had paid even less attention to this "court" than I did to the F Troop. I assumed it was the legal equivalent of miniature golf. It turned out my ass was on the line.

I was charged with three offenses:

1. theft
2. endangering a student
3. disorderly conduct at a university-sanctioned event

If I was convicted on any one of these charges, I was out of school.

I was given a student lawyer to defend me and a trial date for the following September. That was another jolt because by delaying things till the beginning of my senior year, any kind of conviction—even if it was eventually overturned on appeal—would also have killed my football career at Carolina.

The only defense I had was my own testimony. My lawyer thought that might bring me up a little short. Could I produce character witnesses? Sure, I said. I produced Steve Streater, Paul Davis, and Buddy Curry. The lawyer wasn't exactly brimming with confidence and, to tell the truth, neither was I. But my boys, the guys on the football team, were the only people in school who really knew me, and if they couldn't stand up for me, who could?

Whatever hopes I had were riding on Buddy Curry. This guy was one of the great bullshit artists ever. I mean, he could bullshit his way through a minefield blindfolded and walking on his hands. Well, when the day came, we all went over to the court. We sat in a room outside and were called in one by one as we were needed. I was worried, of course; my coaches and friends were even more worried—all attempts at a plea bargain had failed—but I still had this half belief that when Buddy went in he would save the day. They got around to calling him and he went in behind this door. He didn't come out for a long time. When he did, I knew it was all over. He was sweating like they had been sticking needles under his fingernails for an hour. He could hardly bring himself to look at me. He mumbled as he went past: "I tried, man. I did the best I could!"

What he really was saying was that I was going to fry.

I was called last, after Streater and Davis had testified, and when I got into this room I saw that it was set up like a real court with a judge's bench and a witness box and all these official-looking types in three-piece suits fingering papers and legal-looking documents.

The prosecutor really got off on me. He made me sound like I was wanted in sixteen states. The way he ran it down, it was as though I had actually tried to kill this student and steal his property. He kept saying over and over again that I was a huge, powerful football player and the guy I swung at was just a small, frightened student.

All in all, I was in that room for two hours. It turned out the only defense I had was the truth. I told them I didn't steal anything—that I was handed these shirts by a friend to hold—and that it wasn't right of anyone to take the shirts away from me. If someone takes my property, I explained, I would defend myself and my property. I also explained that my only friends were football players, and living and working so hard as a team creates loyalties that are a little out of the ordinary.

I don't know if they were convinced, but after I testified the dean got on the stand and told them that I really couldn't have known she was a dean because, well, she just wasn't dressed like one that day and that in her mind I had been acting on the spur of the moment, not deliberately trying to harm anyone.

They found me not guilty. I was still a Tar Heel football player. If it had gone the other way, my football future would have been in the South Sea Islands or at the North Pole. No other college would have touched me, the NFL surely wouldn't have drafted me, I would have been out a few million dollars.

That had to be the highest miniature golf payoff in history!

THE summer between my junior and senior years was also when I met Ivery Black. Ivery was an agent, and I didn't know him from Adam. I was living over in the south campus with Steve and a couple of other guys—we had been moved there from the north campus because the school wanted to spare us—or themselves—from trouble. The dorm we were in was deserted save for us. We had been quarantined.

One day, this dude shows up. I mean, it was like suddenly he was standing there one afternoon when I woke up from a nap.

"Lawrence Taylor?" he says.

"That's right."

The guy introduced himself and got into his rap. I listened.

"The NCAA doesn't like this sort of thing," he said, "but there's no law preventing me from talking to you before you finish up here."

That didn't seem terribly dangerous.

"I'm listening."

Ivery explained that while he was an agent, he couldn't give me money at that point—he didn't do that with his athletes. His policy was to lend an athlete what he needed till he got drafted, when the money would be repaid.

Exciting.

What he wanted, he said, was to make sure that an athlete really did think of his future in the right way. Living in a dorm wasn't the best idea because there was too much potential trouble around.

"If you live by yourself you won't throw a table or a pail of garbage out a window, if you know what I mean."

Who was this dude, anyway?

"You live off campus in an apartment. You also don't take any jobs. You work on your football drills instead. You spend the months before the draft improving your skills full time. That's your job, that's your future."

He had it all worked out. If I agreed to take him on as my agent, there would be an initial payment of $500. I would live in the dorm until December, getting another $200 a month so I wouldn't have to work. In December, I'd move off campus and my monthly payments would go up to around $350 to cover the added cost of the apartment.

The guy wanted to know how I thought of myself in relation to the draft. I honestly didn't know, although I was hoping to have a good year and go on to the pros. I'd have been happy just to be drafted. Ivery told me that I probably didn't know how good I really was or how high in the draft I would probably go. Those weren't questions I could answer. I had something else on my mind.

"Where's the money?"

That's how our relationship began. Ivery since then has not only been an agent, adviser, and business associate, he's also been a real friend. But at that point, all I knew was the man was standing there with money, and I surely wasn't going to turn down a loan that made my day-to-day life a little easier. We were both probably taking chances with the NCAA, but all of that, frankly, didn't bother me in the least. From day one, I knew why I was in school. Whether I made it or not, I was there to get on with a career in football. The University of North Carolina, like any of the big-time big-money schools in cahoots with the NCAA, was into making

money through football in ways players never dreamed
about.

I have to be straight here. College football is to the pros
what minor-league baseball is to the majors. The NFL gets a
free ride there, of course, because the schools do the work
the league should be paying for. The schools and the NCAA
get a free ride, too, because the millions they make they
don't have to share with the players. The NCAA is into "am-
ateurism." The schools are into academics. Both of them are
full of shit because what they are really into is money. And
it's the players who make the money for them.

Take the NCAA. They have all kinds of standards and
rules that, if they were honestly—rather than selectively—
enforced, would create teams of Phi Beta Kappa students,
very few of whom could play football. Last season, the
NCAA got into this ridiculous thing where they suspended
sixty members of the Nebraska football team for a variety of
infractions—I mean, that was the whole football team! Go
get 'em NCAA! What happened then was that ABC said fine,
but we're not going to pay any money to televise a bunch of
walk-ons in Nebraska football suits. Nebraska had an up-
coming game against Oklahoma, I think, and ABC was telling the NCAA and the schools that, sure, they could go
ahead and play—but not to expect any television revenue in
return. What did the NCAA do? They reinstated the entire
Nebraska team and said they would look into the infractions
later on. In a more celebrated case, they went after S.M.U. for
allowing players to be paid. But when the NCAA lowered
the boom, S.M.U. already was under a TV ban—no lost revenue there—and they acted only because a former player had
gone public with his story about being paid. They *had* to act.

The NCAA and the colleges, because they have this
pious front about academic standards, wind up dogging and
corrupting players left and right. They wink and nod in
some cases, they come down hard in others. They'll get you
for paying athletes in one publicized case but do nothing to

chop down the money tree that keeps everyone but the players well fed. They'll insist on academic "standards," but enforce them only when they need a few headlines or they can't help themselves because somebody's exposed himself—and his school—in public.

I'm in favor of players getting a good general education—not necessarily a specialized, college-level education, but one that gets them through some basics in life. But players are taken into some colleges who don't even have a chance of getting that because they just aren't prepared, while other schools make it so hard to get in and stay in that hundreds, even thousands of the nation's best athletes just don't get the chance to show what they can do. There's a guy I know from home, for example—the best athlete I've ever seen in my life (and I've seen some good ones, believe me). This guy was awesome on a football field but lost in a classroom. Okay, he's nodding on a streetcorner down home today and some pious sonuvabitch in the NCAA will tell you that's proof about having standards. These are the same folks, remember, who say nothing when players who do make it through the football program find that their academic eligibility runs out as soon as they have played their last game for dear old Tech, who leave school with no degree and no pro football contract in hand.

What's the answer? I'm a football player, not an educator—but I'll tell you this: you don't need four years of French and two years of nuclear physics to kick the shit out of a quarterback. If you're Phi Beta Kappa smart, let's face it: the chances are you're not going to go out for football anyway. There's an unofficial double standard for football players where they have to come off like full-time scholars while, in reality, they are full-time athletes working to make millions of dollars for their schools and for the NCAA. Why doesn't the NCAA check out some science or psychology majors, see what they're messing around with in their laboratories when no one is looking? There *should* be a double standard for athletes and regular students, but it should be official and different from the one they have now. It should allow students who are in school for a college education to get it, and athletes who are there to play ball to do it without penalty or obstruction. It would even be better for the NCAA. They could make their millions without coming off like a bunch of hand-wringing hypocrites—while at the same time allowing themselves to be fairer to athletes. They could honorably face up to the fact that football players in college already *are* professionals in terms of what they put out, but amateurs in the sense that four-year "scholarships"—worth about $40,000, or $10,000 per season—come as close as you can get to playing for nothing.

Coaches, like everyone else in the system, are caught up in the mess. Unlike the players, they make plenty of money if they work for schools with big football programs. They have to win if they want to hold on to their paychecks, so they do all sorts of bullshit things to stay within the rules while at the same time making sure they don't let good players get hung before their eligibility runs out. In my school, there were two different head coaches. One was a guy who said damn the torpedoes, full speed ahead. He did everything he could for his players, helping them get by with all the little favors and some of the big ones, like steering them to courses that would give them the best chance of maintaining academic standing. The other coach we had was the opposite. He *believed* in the system to a T. The system, for example, says that a football scholarship lasts as long as a player's eligibility. Eligibility obviously ends with the player's last game for his school. After that—so long, it's been good to know you, graduate if you can. Now, Crum had a literal interpretation for this unwritten rule. After we played our last 1980 game—the Bluebonnet Bowl in Houston—he got pissed off because ten seniors were late for the team bus from the hotel to the airport. He had the bus leave without them and barred them from the plane when they got there on their own, even though takeoff had been delayed for an hour. Was the man a bastard? Nah, he just knew the system.

So did I. I didn't need any freshman orientation book to tell me that any guy in the football program can't deal with an academic program the way regular students can. The rules say a football player is expected to take so many hours, hold such-and-such a grade average, be responsible for all the things other students are responsible for—and then put in sixty hours a week on a football field, do contact drills, study game books, run forties and hundreds, and get up in the morning for a "sunrise run" if he blows a study hall. When you add up all the hours you put into the sport, all the bullshit you have to take from coaches and teachers and administrators and officials from the NCAA, it's obviously not worth it. But that's the only way you can make it if you want to go to the pros.

My answer to all that was simple: If you can't change the system—and who could?—you better learn how to beat it. I did. There were a number of courses that were ready-made for football players. You know, large lecture classes, twelve hundred people or more, with two tests—a midterm and a final—both multiple-choice. Shit. In those courses, you're gonna get what the guy sitting next to you gets. The only thing you have to do is remember not to copy the same name on your paper. but there are only so many of these courses.

I did take some courses I cared about and learned things from, but that didn't get me through school. I learned every little bit I could about how things worked, and I took advantage of them. The rules, for example, said I had to take a full schedule of so many hours. I took half loads and made sure I had a good supply of add and drop cards, properly dated, for the end of the semester. Then I'd go around the school during exam week looking for those courses where 100 percent of the grade was based on that final exam. I'd sit next to somebody I knew, copy his paper, and hand in mine while slipping an add card into the pile of papers before I left the room. Simple. Any fool could grab a C that way.

I bailed some friends out, too. One friend was going to be thrown out of school because he had flunked three out of his five courses. I dragged him up to the dean's office and argued for him that there had been some terrible mistake: The courses he had flunked, he had actually dropped—there were properly dated drop cards to prove it. And what was more, there were three other courses—courses he had passed—that apparently had been overlooked. There were add cards to prove that as well! Fifteen minutes after we got to the dean's office, my friend was back in school, his average having risen dramatically in the process.

When I think of it now, I have such mixed feelings about all of that. I surely am pissed off by ballplayers who go to college, accept money under the table from alumni or from no-show jobs, and then, after it's over, get on their moral high horse and turn the school in. If people feel that way, the time to get it out is while they're in school. Afterward doesn't count. It's like trying to clear your conscience when what you're really doing is looking to make a name for yourself.

On the other hand, the system is a total fraud. It doesn't start in college, either. It starts way back when kids aren't given a decent way to develop those kinds of study habits and skills needed to cope with a college program and the life that comes afterward. The colleges aren't responsible for that one; society is and families are.

But a football player, in his way, is as specialized as a law student or a medical student. The effort he puts into football is every bit as time-consuming and draining. And as far as I know, there are no law students out there running sets of forties.

Most athletes who go to college on athletic scholarships are there because that is the only way they can beat a life of poverty and drudgery. Very few of them will ever get to the pros—as only a percentage of medical students will ever become doctors. But that doesn't mean that a top athlete, one who does have a chance to make it, should be penalized by the academic system. It doesn't mean that a lesser athlete should be punished, either. Athletes are used by the schools for their own money-making purposes and should be paid, not punished, for the rewards they bring their schools. And then if athletes want to turn around and go to school and get all that academics has to offer, good for them. Otherwise, cut the shit and get on with the game. The way things stand now, cheating is inevitable, and only a fool or a man on the make would get on his high horse about it.

Our team really came around in my senior year. We went 11–1, won the ACC, finished something like sixth in the national polls, and had the number-one-ranked defense in the nation. I don't think we allowed a touchdown until the eighth week of the season. Our guys up front—the line and linebackers—were dubbed "The Magnificent Seven." I played well every game. My name started to hit the papers, and I could feel my confidence building from week to week. I can't really describe the feeling I came to have—it was like nothing I had known before. I had this sense that anything that was thrown at me I could handle. And then it got to the point where I started to free-lance.

If I was supposed to cover, I'd rush. If I was supposed to rush, sometimes I'd cover. I started really being able to read things, and I had this ability to turn mistakes into big plays. I came to believe in that basic part of my game then.

I was a co-captain on the team and very much my own person. My friend and teammate Paul Davis says I was a "quiet leader" who led by example, but that when I talked, people listened. PD said that if I ever spoke in the huddle, people buttoned up their chin straps. I don't know about that, but I do know that I used to get on people if I felt they weren't doing their jobs—particularly the secondary. Davis says I let them know that we were doing our job up front and that they had better do theirs back of us. All I knew was whatever the differences in talent, there never was any excuse for not giving all of yourself—mentally and physically—on game day. If you blew a play because your mind was somewhere else, the hell with you, get off the field. If you saw a damn play in front of you and didn't do much about it, why were you out there in the first place?

I think a lot of us on the defense had this attitude. Nine out of eleven guys on the defensive unit and seven more on the offense were seniors from the days of Bill Dooley. We just got tighter and tighter as a team, even when Dick Crum made things tougher and tougher. I decided—we decided—that the team was ours. We decided we were just going to take some things in our own hands that we had held back on before.

We started going to Crum and telling him what we would do and what we wouldn't do. There were times when Crum called a practice when no one felt like practicing. We'd tell him, "No practice today."

He'd get on me because I chased instead of dropped on a certain play. I didn't give a shit. I told him, "Why wait and do it according to the book when you smell something else?" What he wanted were Xs and Os. His playbook didn't have anything about heart. We took care of business on Saturday afternoons.

I fought with the staff all the time, too. I remember one time a group of us decided to take a little time off to go fishing. Steve, Paul, Donnell, Tyrus, and I went out one afternoon and caught forty or so brim and had us a little fish fry—to go with a few cases of beer. We got to this team study hall a little late and a little mellow—and one of the coaches, the strength and conditioning coach, started in on me.

I didn't get nasty with the man, but I said a few things back to him. He told me, "If you can't follow the rules, just get the hell out."

"No problem," I said. I packed up my books and started to leave the study hall.

He followed me outside and suddenly grabbed me by the collar and threw me against a wall. "Who the hell do you think you are?" he said.

How could I possibly answer him? The guy had tripped a wire that threw me right back to the Saturday night fights. I took the sonuvabitch off me and pinned him to a wall and would have killed him if my friends hadn't broken it up.

In all the trouble I ever had with my coaches, I never felt I was doing anything other than being myself—and never going at anyone unless I felt they had unfairly gone at me first. My head coach thought differently. He tried to do something about it—and couldn't. But the payoff for him wasn't anything *I* did, it was what *he* did to the Carolina football program. He took a good program, lived on it for a while, got a ten-year contract out of it—and has been nowhere ever since. None of it had to do with his football knowledge, which was pretty good. Just this idea that the rules would give him what his understanding of people didn't.

By the end of my senior year, I was a consensus All-American. I had played hard, had some good stats—sixty-nine solo tackles and sixteen sacks—but I think what caught people's eye was an ability I had to make "big" plays. (More about "big plays" later.)

At any rate, because I was now an All-American, I started getting around some. I still wasn't known that much outside the ACC, so I wasn't thinking too much about what position I might have in the draft. At that point, I would have been happy just to get the opportunity to play in the pros. When I went out to these banquets around the country for the All-American team, I used to get kind of quiet listening to all the fuss and hoopla. I never thought any of it had really to do with me. I wanted to drink and have a good time.

I remember one dinner in particular, the Kodak All-American banquet. I was there with all these guys I had heard about and read about in the papers. I was in this room drinking and I was sitting near E. J. Junior and Hugh Green, the two most well-known college linebackers in the country then. We were all talking and the guys got around to trying to figure which linebacker would go first in the draft. I remember E.J. saying that Hugh would probably be picked and then he would go second. I think Hugh might have put it just the reverse—but I felt really strange. My name never came up. I sat there wondering whether or not I really belonged in the room with these people. I knew these guys were real stars—and when it came down to it, I didn't know for sure where I fit in.

On the other hand, Ivery seemed to know. He kept telling me that I was going to go higher in the draft than I imagined. He wasn't talking about first round only but about first four or five in the nation! I didn't know what to make of that, either. I started paying some attention, though, when my name started coming up in these magazine articles about the draft, some of which had me going early.

I tended not to believe too much. I wasn't much for accolades in those days and am not now. But I did think plenty about my future. Maybe even too much. After the Bluebonnet Bowl game in my senior year, I was contacted by another agent. This was a guy who knew Ivery well, a "friend" of his, so I thought it wouldn't be harmful to listen to him. I didn't know what I was really worth out there other than what Ivery hinted at.

I got taken to this big glittery party in Houston. It was something to see, believe me. Only in Texas. I never saw so many beautiful women in one place in my life before that night. There was just *everything* there—and before I left for home, I had put my name on a contract with this agent who had arranged it all.

The only thing was that on the plane home, I thought

about what I had done. I thought about Ivery, whose offer to me was never separate from his friendship. Because the football season had ended, I was free to sign with any agent. The arrangement I had with Ivery and the office he worked with didn't go past my senior year. I realized that I had no business doing what I had done. I told Ivery what had happened and that that wasn't me. He didn't get mad or excited, but he did get down to Houston as close to the speed of light as he could go. He got things straightened out. But he didn't feel all that secure about me. He packed his bags and actually moved on up to Chapel Hill to stay with me till draft day and beyond—when I would sign my first pro contract. He arrived at the door of my apartment one afternoon and said he was moving in. That was fine.

He was a pretty good pool player. He taught me how to play golf and a nasty card game called 500.

He also did most of the cooking—and tried like hell to make sure I stayed out of trouble till I cleared out of Chapel Hill.

Why not? With me, anything was possible.

WITH the draft on the horizon, Ivery was all over me like a mother hen. I was chosen to play in the East-West Shrine game and the Japan Bowl game that year—but he was against my participating in either of them. Injury could wreck things for me faster than anything, he said. He was full of stories about athletes who had blown opportunities for big contracts by mangling a knee or a shoulder in a meaningless All-Star game. I wanted to play in the Shrine game. It was an honor. But I also believed Ivery. When I was asked before the game if I wouldn't mind letting Rickey Jackson and E. J. Junior start ahead of me—they were linebackers and cocaptains of the team—I said fine, it was just an honor to be there. I went in later. I played for a little less than a quarter and, following Ivery's suggestion, came out limping with an "injured" foot. To this day Ivery swears that I overdid it, because all he remembers is how the TV cameras picked me up on the sidelines smiling and joking with everyone.

I was a little smarter about the Japan Bowl. I didn't go.

As draft day approached, Ivery was sure I was going to be picked number one or two. We talked about what teams I would like to go to. New Orleans had the first pick in the draft that year, and the Giants had the second.

I said I wanted to go to Dallas. Dallas was the team everybody knew about—and also one of their players was a "home boy," Ron Springs. Ron had played for the Williamsburg Jaycees and for Lafayette High just before me. It would have been something for two of Melvin Jones's projects to line up on the same team in the NFL together.

Ivery wanted me to think more about what was really coming—the Saints or the Giants. I had no preference between them.

I knew nothing about the Giants and not too much more about the Saints (in fact, until I set foot on an NFL field, I had never even been to a professional football game). Ivery made arrangements for me to go down to New Orleans with him to meet Bum Phillips, the Saints' coach. Bum had a reputation of being something of a wild guy and a good guy to play for, and when I met him it was clear he was thinking very seriously about drafting me. He was also interviewing George Rogers, whom the Saints eventually chose. The defensive coaches wanted me, he said, and the offensive coaches wanted Rogers. Bum held the trump card—but he wasn't yet ready to show it.

On the evening before the draft, a group of us went to a Chapel Hill hangout called He's Not Here. The place got its name because it has a pay phone on the wall near the bar and the owner thought it would be the funniest thing in the world if the usual greeting was to pick up the phone and say "He's not here" before the person on the other end had a chance to say "Hello."

At any rate, the guys—Steve, Donnell, and a couple of other seniors—all expected to be drafted the next day. No matter what happened, it was going to be a big day for all of us, and we were there to celebrate—and maybe hide whatever nerves we all shared.

The owner of the place saw us come in and sit down in the garden area, where there were outside tables. He had a round of free beers brought to our table—and then another. He was a Carolina football fan.

After we used up our house credit, we got down to some

serious beer drinking on our own. A big mug in those days cost twenty-five cents. You bought beer by the mug because it turned out to be cheaper than buying it by the pitcher. By the time we finished that night, our bill was $75—or three hundred mugs of beer among six or seven guys.

Now, the thing about alcohol consumption at that rate is that your mind stops having thoughts and starts running TV cartoons instead. And one of the cartoons we were all into—except for Ivery—was how funny beer mugs looked when they went crashing against a wall. After the third or fourth or seventh or eighth round, we started taking our empty beer mugs and throwing them against a nearby wall. People started moving away from us, and Ivery started going crazy.

"The owner's gonna call the cops! What are you guys doing?"

Ivery was thinking of me particularly.

"Man, you're not throwing beer mugs, you're throwing away your careers!"

"Lighten up, Ivery."

We were just having a great old time.

Then the owner came down and saw what was going on. Ivery looked sick. The owner pulled up a chair but didn't say anything. He had this weird look on his face. We were too far gone to care what he might do. He picked up a beer mug, drank it down, and then got into the act himself. He sat there with us the rest of the night firing beer mugs against the wall. More people than you would imagine are into cartoons.

When Ivery got me back to the apartment, it must have been two-thirty or three in the morning. It was hot as a sonuvabitch, and as it was only a few hours till the draft, I decided to park myself right in front of my door and take in the morning breezes.

"Man, you got to get some sleep!" Ivery said.

"Sleep right here," I said.

"You've got to be ready for the draft!"

"I am."

Ivery thought it was nerves, but I know it wasn't, because I was numb—that is, hot and numb. I knew where I slept wouldn't change my position in the draft one iota. So why not in the evening cool? Last thing I remembered before seeing daylight again was Ivery just standing there looking sort of worn and helpless.

I went out like a light—sitting bolt upright.

A few hours later we all went over to watch the draft at this lineman's house. He had one of the few cable hookups around. When the first name was called and it was George Rogers, I got up and said, "All right, no problem," and I went out to the kitchen to get a beer. I did know that sometimes players who were supposed to go high in the draft didn't go till the second or third round. But I wasn't ready to panic just yet. I got my brew and slowly ambled on back to catch the rest of the proceedings. The problem was that during this little intermission, I had been picked by the New York Giants. I never saw the actual moment, though I had gone through oceans of beer and stayed up half the night in anticipation. I wasn't disappointed in the least. I felt relieved. The guys congratulated me, I thanked them and was going to head straight back to my apartment, but before I got out the door, Linda was on the phone. She had been good and pissed at me because I didn't take her along the night before and didn't invite her to watch the draft show with me, and she said that I needed to hurry back because I was going to get a call from the Giants in ten minutes.

When I got home, sure enough, Coach Ray Perkins called. He wanted to know if I could get up to New York that day and I said that I would. I was on a plane that afternoon—with Ivery—and by day's end, after I had met the staff and team officials, I was in a hotel suite near the Meadowlands. The next morning I was scheduled to meet the New York press.

I don't remember too much about that first press conference except that I tried to be as low-key as I could. I'm told I said something about liking New York already because they ran the Three Stooges on the local channels. Sounds like something I would say, but I know that I couldn't share with the press some of what I was really feeling.

On the drive from Newark Airport to Giants Stadium that first day, I couldn't believe how ugly everything looked and smelled. The stadium itself, when it rolled by the window, was this big blob of cement rising out of a swamp with a lot of roads running around it. Later on, when I finally signed my first contract, I remember looking out the window of the car as I drove away from the stadium, thinking, "I have to be here for six years, somebody's got to be kidding!" Where I came from and where I had gone to school, there were always trees and grass and open spaces around the football fields I played on—and the only smells other than the sweet air came from the sweat of the game.

There were other things going on as well. For one, Ivery had sent the Giants a telegram before the draft, asking them not to pick me. It was a negotiating ploy on his part, because he knew there was no way the Giants were going to pass on me or trade away my rights if they really wanted me. There was no rival league at that point, and an incoming player had little bargaining power.

But we were going to ask for a lot of money—a lot for those days—and there had been stories in the New York papers that if I got anything like the money my agent had been talking about, veteran players on the Giants would ask to be traded. I wasn't excited about that, but I meant it when I said I would rather play for a team where people weren't mad at me. For sure, I wasn't about to tell my agent to have them pay me less.

And then, also, I was someone from a small town whose idea of a big town had been Chapel Hill. New York was just so different from anything I had known, I knew from the first second I saw the place that all bets were off. This was going to be a place where I was going to be on my own, like it or not—and I didn't like it at all when I was up there having to play Mr. Cool before the New York press.

The main thing was that I really knew nothing about the New York Giants. I knew nothing about their traditions, their players, their ideas about the game of football. I couldn't have picked out a big star from a shooting star. Everyone wore shoulder pads and shoes. I was neither awed nor afraid. Just alone.

The thing was, I was determined to do well, to work hard, learn as quickly as I could, do everything possible to gain the respect of my peers. It wasn't easy leaving Carolina when my friend Steve was lying paralyzed in a hospital, and there was much of my life down there that still hadn't been quite worked out.

When I went up to New York, Linda was six months pregnant and our plans were eventually to get married—but not just yet. That past January, when I was in San Francisco for the Shrine game, I bought her an engagement ring. She met me at the airport when I returned from Frisco, and I just tossed her this little box when I walked up to her.

I said, "Here." That was my romantic way of proposing.

But we still hadn't set a date. And a lot of my friends were telling me that marriage and the wild life of the NFL just did not mix.

The first real experience I had with the team was at veterans' camp later that spring. The only guy I had ever heard of on the Giants was Brad Van Pelt, and he was one of the guys the press had been saying was going to be asking out if I wound up getting more money than he did—which I did. He didn't have anything to say to me that day, or for a while afterward. Aside from the other rookies, the only veteran player on the Giants who tried to befriend me was Harry Carson—and that first meeting, for me, turned out to be memorable.

After practice that day, Harry took me out for dinner. We

went to a nearby Beefsteak Charlie's. I don't remember the food or the conversation—except that I felt glad an older player was paying some attention to me. Harry was a cool guy, a good talker, and someone I knew even then was a take-charge person on the field. When Harry talked, you listened. When he moved, you paid attention.

After dinner Harry and I went back to the hotel the team was staying in. When we got to the lobby, instead of going off in different ways, Harry said to me, "Listen, something's going on." He motioned for me to follow him. I did. I hadn't the foggiest idea what he meant. We got to this room—I still had no clue. Then he opened the door to the room and motioned me in. I followed him.

There was this girl in the room—call her a dancing girl. She seemed quite pleased to be there—and so did the three or four other players from the team who were in there, too.

Man, was this what the NFL was all about?

I know this: This wasn't in my playbook. I'm a free-lancer, yeah, but I was just a little bit shy in this situation. Call me rookie.

In any case, by the time I finally moved to New York for the opening of training camp, I had a better idea of who the New York Giants were. They weren't nearly as crazy as that friendly introduction to life in the NFL would have you believe. The Giants did have their hell-raisers, but frankly the team was nothing like the Raiders, who have had this reputation for years of six days of craziness along with pulverizing opponents on the Lord's Day. The Giants had been losing forever and were something like a bus station, with guys moving in and out all the time. You have to stay in one place for a while to earn a reputation for hell-raising. The Carolina team I came from had more crazies on it than any Giants team I've played for.

But my main goal then wasn't to prove I was nuts. I knew I was going to work hard, play hard, and keep my mouth shut. I moved all the stuff I had from Newark Airport right up to Pleasantville, went through the swamps and the gas fields. Nothing had changed. At Pace College, where we trained, there was a dormitory room waiting for me. It had nothing in it—just a small bed for me and one for my room-mate, who turned out to be Byron Hunt.

I think because of the time I had spent with Harry, I felt a little more like I belonged than I might have. There were a lot of guys who seemed to resent me. But either way, it didn't really matter. I knew why I was there.

After we won the Super Bowl last season, books and articles about the Giants got rushed into print. Here was something I picked up about that first camp I was in:

> Ray Perkins, the head coach, liked to conduct a rookie scrimmage just before the veterans were scheduled to report, and because this kid who would soon be known as LT had drawn so much notice, many of the veterans showed up a day early to watch the quasi-game. They were stunned. On one play, LT rushed into the backfield from a position best described as wide defensive end. The play was going away from him, a sweep to the other side.
>
> He caught the runner in the backfield.
>
> Four times he sacked the quarterback that after-noon, and he made eleven tackles, and all during his bravura performance, the hardened veterans cheered. [*Big Blue: A Giant Year* by Dave Klein]

What I recall from that afternoon was just doing what came naturally. I played with enthusiasm—like a lot of other new players. I did just what I did in college. I don't know about cheering veterans—the same number who weren't talking to me before that scrimmage weren't talking to me afterward.

I had a job to do.

Most evenings that first year I spent studying my play-book. I was lucky because the Giants were putting in a new defensive system—we had been 4–3, we now were going to 3–4—and everybody was really starting from scratch, vet-erans along with rookies. The staff gave you time. Each day you'd get a handful of plays to study, which they'd run the following day in practice. If you messed up, that was okay—as long as you didn't do it again. There were guys on that team, you could pick 'em right out—Brian Kelly, for one—who knew *everything*. That impressed the hell out of me.

I didn't get along with Byron, my roommate, in those first few weeks. It seemed like he used to fuss about all kinds of things. He had the damn TV on all the time, even when we went to sleep. That used to drive me crazy. It was hard enough studying with the thing on, but it was pure torture trying to go to sleep to it. As it was my set, not his, I felt like I had a right to shut it off. There were some occasions when I got out of bed, told Byron that I'd be damned if that TV was gonna stay on, and I'd just switch it off. He'd get pissed at that and we'd get into it a little.

It was tough for Byron then. He was a linebacker, like I was. He had been been picked far down in the draft, and there wasn't too much press or talk about him coming into camp—but he was a hell of a player, and he rightfully be-lieved he was as good as I was or anyone else. He was my roommate, but both of us were always aware that we were in competition for the same job on the team.

The last week of camp, we started getting along better. He had made the squad and he was looking for a place to stay and I asked him to come on and live with us. Dave Young, another rookie, and I had rented a house together and we had plenty of room. Byron accepted. Linda, at that time, was still attending school in Carolina.

I have to admit New York City was like no place I had ever seen before. I mean, it was huge and strange and impersonal—and there were all these stories you heard. For a while, I had seen it only from a distance—from a plane window or a car window. I didn't think too much about it while I was living and working up in Pleasantville during camp. It was just there—like death and taxes. One day we had a day off and a group of us decided to go down to New York and take a look for ourselves.

We were all young players, mostly first-year men, and we didn't know anybody down there. We were just looking to have a good time. We went down to Forty-second Street—I mean, isn't that where you go in New York?

We walked up and down the street, hardly believing what we saw. There were all these peep shows and derelicts and noise and lights. I had never seen anything like it. There were marquees that said "Live Sex Shows." Try that one on if you come from Lightfoot, Virginia! I mean, I just couldn't believe they'd have something like this in the middle of the street. We decided to see for ourselves.

We went into this darkened theater, walked down to the first row, and took a seat. No one knew us, of course, and for sure we didn't know anyone. The place was fully of seedy, weird-looking types. Up on the stage this girl was just dancing around. We sat there watching and then this guy makes his entrance on the stage, goes up to the girl, carries her over to a bed, and just bangs her. Nothing fancy. Just banged her—in front of this roomful of derelicts.

Because we had been in camp for only two or three weeks and didn't know the city and weren't yet people who would be recognized by anyone, we could walk up and down Forty-second Street without being embarrassed, just taking in the street. We went to another place afterward; I don't remember how they advertised except that it was in lights and had plenty of pictures. We went upstairs. There was a desk and a big room. If you paid ten bucks, you could walk around looking at these different women. The ten bucks was just for the look. If you found someone to your liking, you made your own arrangements and went off into one of these little cubicles in the back.

I paid my ten bucks and walked around, looking. But there wasn't anyone there who struck my fancy. But a couple of the guys actually connected and so the rest of us waited around—for a long time.

When we got back to camp, it was morning. The coaches had their whistles around their necks and their clipboards in their hands. We were in our party clothes, they were in their work suits. We might not have been the Raiders, but we were all young, strong Giants. We made practice on time, ready to go.

10

I wasn't particularly awed by the Giants or by the NFL. I had played before big crowds, crazy crowds, against good competition and sophisticated offenses long enough to feel that I could hold my own in the pros. Which isn't to say I was totally arrogant about it, either.

The New York Giants' playbook weighs approximately eight pounds and seems to contain as many plays as there are names in the New York phone book. You have defensive formations and variations with names like "Stack," "Fire," "Mustang," "Lion"; stunt and game calls (defensive changes in the line of scrimmage) like "Green Read," "Loop," "Stuff," "Tess," "Me," "You," etc.

I broke my brains trying to memorize that stuff, hated it, couldn't do it. It took me three years to finally get most of it down where it felt comfortable—and the damn thing is the "bible" of the system. You just know, someone like me—who burns on instinct—is going to have trouble fifty different ways.

I made more errors that first year than I can possibly count. The trouble was, someone else was counting. The Giants have a little internal stat call M.E.s—mental errors. I made more of them than anyone on the team in my rookie year. My attitude was screw it, let me play.

I know that if I was another kind of player, I might have

been gone. You get tested on the playbook every week in the pros. The Giants do it, most teams do it. A lot of players who have the physical ability but who consistently flunk these playbook tests wind up getting cut. I was lucky, I wasn't. I had a coach who recognized what I could do.

In these early weeks and months, my game was instinct—raw and simple. Do everything full speed, improvise, free-lance, kick butt, and take no prisoners. The difference between my rookie year on the Giants and my freshman year at Carolina—apart from the fact that I was bigger, stronger, and more experienced—was that I wasn't at all confused about where you got respect. Even though I felt it was not my place to open my mouth a lot, I was the same person I always was. On the football field, there was one and only one way to prove it.

I played all out every minute, every day—not only in games but in practice, too. That was maybe crazier than anything I could have been doing off the field. I mean, I was into making war on guys who regularly threw 250 pounds of high-explosive speed at you. I didn't care. Let me at them.

Most experienced pros don't think this way at all—for sure, I learned differently over time. In the pros, just because the hitting is so hard on Sundays, you try to hold it down and go half speed during the week. I mean, why fill up the hospitals with your own?

I used to go after anyone who was willing to challenge me. We had a second-year fullback named Leon Perry, a big, bruising sonuvabitch who didn't know from half speed either. I mean, you took one look into Leon's eyes and you knew this man, no matter how nice he was off the field, had a few screws loose. He hit you—in practice—like he wanted to kill you. So you could say we were meant for each other—in the same way two cars in a head-on collision are meant for each other.

For a while, it seemed like Leon was hell-bent on destroying my roommate, Byron Hunt. The Giants regularly ran a practice variation of the Dallas 36 Lead, where the tight end blocks down and the fullback comes on to cream the outside linebacker, opening the way for Tony Dorsett. It seemed like one week, our offense just kept running this play at Byron. Leon would slam into Byron, and Byron— who loves hitting as much as anyone—would let Leon have it right back. Leon came after him play after play. Bam! Bam! Bam! On impact, Leon's helmet would get pushed down, gashing the bridge of his nose. Leon didn't mind. A few days of this and Byron was out with a shoulder injury. And then Leon turned his crazy eyes and big body on me. That was fine. I turned my crazy eyes and big body right back on him.

I don't count what followed in days—just by the measure of one play. Leon Perry hit me so hard on this one play, I felt my wristbands pop off. Byron and I both went to him and we sort of called a truce.

Meanwhile, I practiced just as hard. I wasn't about to let up, do anything at half speed. One day Bill Parcells, who was the defensive coordinator then, came up to me and told me to take it easy or I'd be wrecked before the end of my first year.

I couldn't do it, though. I left the field with a headache after that collision with Leon Perry. I left the field with a headache after every practice and every game that year.

Speaking of Bill, he used to ride me pretty regularly in those early days. I know I wasn't alone; Bill was—and is—a needler. He will pick, pick, pick, sometimes in fun, sometimes seriously; he's a guy who knows how to motivate, and he'll mess with your head to do it. Like a lot of the coaches, he didn't quite take to my free-lancing ways. As far as he was concerned, an error was an error. It seemed like every day he would let me know that. He'd march out on the field, yell at me after a play, march back, come out, yell at me again. I'd hear him on the sidelines, his hands cupped to his mouth, ragging me almost as if I was the only other person out there besides himself. Finally I just couldn't take it.

He had said something to me from way across the field and I turned toward him, yelling at the top of my lungs: "You get the fuck off my back! You don't like the way I play, put in Skorupan [John Skorupan had been the right outside linebacker the year before]! You can trade me, you can cut me, you can sit me down, but just get the fuck off my back!"

The practice came to a dead stop. You could suddenly hear the silence fall over the field. I mean, I had gone off on the man—and you just didn't do that. I didn't give a shit. Giants coaches were the same as coaches anywhere. I couldn't have cared less that this was my rookie year or that this was the NFL—or that someone might actually take me up on my demand to be cut or left alone.

Nobody said a word to me. Not our head coach, none of the other players—and not Bill himself. Bill just stopped ragging me after that. Well, maybe he changed his tactics. He's never one to quit anything. Once it was clear that we were going to be friends, not enemies, he just switched to the indirect approach. During a film session one day, I noticed that he started drawing attention to the play of an outside linebacker on another team. He was real cool about it. He didn't let on that he was trying to correct anyone about anything.

I remember, in particular, that we were watching some Tampa Bay film—we were going to play them later in that year—and he stopped the camera because he saw something that interested him.

"Did you see that, that number what's-his-name—that Hugh Green? Let's see that play again." This just happened to be the same Hugh Green who dogged my pre-draft All-American banquet days.

We saw that play over again. And then again—and then day after day after day. And during each playing of the Tampa Bay film, Bill would stop it with this innocent-sounding jive about how good Hugh Green was—as though his only possible motive was appreciation of the guy's skill.

I don't know whether it was the fifth or the twentieth time, but finally I said—in the dark, with the film going and Bill doing the same old number—"Bill, if you think the guy's so fucking good, why didn't you draft him?"

The place cracked up and Bill finally ditched those old Hugh Green movies for new ways to needle me.

I don't know why I didn't learn the playbook faster. I don't think it had anything to do with aptitude, because if I see something once, I've got it—my memory is excellent. Normally I can look at a page once and give it right back to you. I did it all the time when studying in school—or copying other people's papers. On a football field, you fool me once with a play, you better not try it a second time—it's written up there in stone.

I know it wasn't lack of respect or concern on my part, either. I remember that when I was shown the Giants' defenses for the first time, my reaction was that no other team could possibly be that sophisticated and advanced.

The best answer I can come up with for the "difficulty" I was having was that, hell, it was just me being me. I didn't then—and don't now—believe in "the book." You do everything by the book and you wind up losing something. The coaches had a word then—"uptempo"—which was meant to describe actual game play as opposed to pregame play in the NFL. "Uptempo" was really the only thing that separated college from pro play as far as I was concerned, the only thing I hadn't been fully prepared for. It was simply the tremendous speed of the game. How could you stand there figuring out plays to yourself when the action was on you suddenly in a blur? Hell, that was the action I *craved*, too. I wasn't going to be left out of it. And all the while I knew that what I did—right or wrong—would put me in the middle of it.

The thing is that my body, my energy, is simply high-speed and overwound. It's like I can't keep up with myself. I'm impatient, I have to be going all the time, off the field as well as on. It's like I can't burn off enough energy.

I remember in those days that after morning practice, when we'd break for lunch, I'd go directly to the basketball court. After practice in the afternoon, I'd return to the basketball court. When I finished at the court, I'd grab a bite to eat and then maybe I'd go on to a bowling alley. I mean, I just couldn't stop. The guys on the team must have thought I was really nuts. Sometimes it felt like I was just sitting there inside myself watching this big unstoppable force—me—crashing around in the outside world.

I know that if I didn't play the way I did, there wouldn't be anything to talk about. But I did play that way. Speed and power will cover a multitude of mistakes and sometimes convert those mistakes into advantages. The Giants' playbook today has incorporated several of my early "mistakes" into playbook pages. I love it. Check out the "Stack 2 Double Hard." Sounds a little like nuclear physics, doesn't it? It was just me on a busted play busting some quarterback's head. Looks good in the big blue book.

I wasn't brash or insulting or cocky to anybody in my rookie year. I didn't feel I had anything made, I wasn't looking to prove anything or live up to anything—except on a football field. I was just myself, and at that time I didn't see why playing for the Giants should have been any different from playing for the Tar Heels.

My roommates and I got along really well. We went everywhere and did everything together. Both Dave Young and Byron were free spirits like myself. We'd drink, play pool, party, tear around all the time. Because I was a first-round draft pick, some corporation provided a lease deal on a car for me, which I shared with my roommates. Sometimes we'd go on into the city looking for exciting things to do—and we'd get lost. I'd drive around these city streets not having the faintest idea of where we were or where we were going, knowing only that I was going fast.

One night, coming home from a round of bars when all of us were pretty ripped, I came up our street and as we approached our house, I gunned our car right up the front lawn into a tree. Did it deliberately.

"Taylor, hey, what's happening?" my roomies said.

I backed the car up out into the street, then gunned it up onto the lawn into the tree all over again! Let me at 'em!

We played pool a lot. Dave Young and I got into these hairy nine-ball matches—which I usually won—and I had Dave owing me $5,000 over that year.

Then there was Byron. We played one night and he beat me. I don't like to lose at anything. When Byron beat me, I wanted a rematch right away—but he didn't want to give me the chance. You don't do that, you just don't do that!

"Come on, Byron, right now: your contract against my contract!"

He looked at me like he didn't know whether I was kidding or not.

I wasn't. I didn't care. I would have bet six years and a million bucks to get even.

Byron, like any sane man, put up his pool cue. I couldn't talk or intimidate him into changing his mind, so eventually we went back to drinking and having a good time.

For both of us, nothing we did during the week ever interfered with what we had to do on Sundays. On the other hand, Dave often did better at nighttime playing than game-day playing.

I don't know what it was about him, maybe because he was a second-round draft choice and figured he had things made, but he seemed to forget that he had to work hard. He put on too much weight, he ambled around in practices, he eventually played himself right off the Giants.

Perk, who demanded blood and guts from his players,

got all over Dave's ass. I mean, you don't play lazy for this man. He started to run Dave to death in practice. The guy was a physical specimen—6-6 and 220 pounds—but Perk couldn't have cared less. He told Byron and me one day to kick Dave's ass every time we could—he was lined up against the outside linebackers and was a natural target. And we wound up hitting him with everything.

Off the field, Dave wanted to know what was wrong, wanted to pull a truce. All we could do was shrug. Perk was the coach, and he was determined to change Dave or wear his ass out and run him off. Dave was cut the following year.

I was accepted slowly by the older players, only after it was clear I was out there to play as hard as anyone on the team. These older players, especially the linebackers, were great players, had lived through many losing years without too much to show. Some of them, independent of any contract problems they were having when I arrived, weren't about to fall on their faces before any rookie.

It was a card game—Bouree—that broke the ice. On long road trips—to the West Coast—some of the guys would get a game of Bouree going on the plane. The game was a natural betting game—whoever took the most books in a round won a pot. It was perfect for me; watch me go. When I dropped a hundred bucks in one run, I couldn't wait for more. I was all right as far as the guys were concerned.

"Hey, Taylor, come on over!" they'd yell every time we got on a plane after that. Eventually I was just one of eight or nine guys—including Phil and Bill and Jimmy and Brad and Brian—who just bet their asses on anything in a card deck. Hell, we'd drop money on the table, a mound of it, then cut the deck for the high card winner.

Some time after this first Bouree game, I don't recall exactly when, I was sitting in a bar and the waitress suddenly put down a drink in front of me. "The people at that table wanted you to have this," she said. She pointed to a table where Brad Van Pelt and Brian Kelly were sitting.

"What is it?" I asked.

"A kamikaze," she said. I had never heard of the drink and to this day don't know what's in it. It went down like its name—right through the smokestack and *wham!*

For a while after that, Brad and Brian used to communicate with me just that way. We'd all be in a bar and they'd send over a kamikaze—like it was a calling card or a challenge, I'm not sure which. Every time I got one of those bad boys, I'd knock it down. Then, finally, instead of having an individual drink put down before me, the guys'd have whole pitchers of the stuff sent over. As I said, show me good linebackers and I'll show you some strange mental profiles.

Brad and Brian. They were really a pair. They were intense, hard-nosed players on the field, and they were wild men off the field, especially Brad. We had to be friends.

These guys were the ones who first took me out to Foley's, the team hangout in Pleasantville, during camp, and they were the ones who eventually took me over to The Bench, a bar and go-go place near Giants Stadium. I've gotten a lot of flack over the years—including having my phone bugged to the present day—because I wound up making friends with the guy who ran The Bench, a guy who's supposed to have a nasty background. But from day one, I was always treated fairly and courteously over there. For sure, none of my troubles ever stemmed from The Bench. When the Giants started to pressure me about it, I would tell different club officials, including Bill, "Hey, I'm on my way to The Bench. Want to come along?"

With Brad and Brian, I was in good hands. The transition from Carolina to the pros was as smooth as it could be. The only real difference was that instead of Franklin Street there was the biggest playground in the world—New York City.

Here comes number 56. Watch out!

11

THERE are three types of people in the world: those who watch things happen, those who make things happen, and those who don't know what's happening. I like to think I'm the type who makes things happen.

That wasn't always easy when you made as many errors as I did in my first year. There was one home game when I blew a play and Brian, who knew the playbook so well he wound up coaching the coaches, reamed me out in front of 75,000 people. That was no joke. I was shocked and hurt—but I had it coming.

But I wouldn't trade my first year for anything. A lot of rookies look to their first year full of fear and pressure. I surely wanted to succeed, but I had another feeling about being a rookie: It is the only season you ever have where you don't have to live up to anything you've done before. Just go out and do it. It's the one time you will be judged on the basis of what you do rather than who you were.

I had my rookie moments like anyone else. There was a preseason game at Three Rivers Stadium against the Steelers. I remember getting goose bumps when some of the Steelers—Mean Joe Greene, Jack Lambert, that front four of theirs—were being introduced. The week we went down to play Dallas, I remember feeling jumpy. Dallas had been my pop's team when I was growing up; Ron Springs, a "home boy" from Lafayette, played for them; and Tony Dorsett was supposed to be one of my weekend targets. Harry Carson warned me as we prepared not to be awed down there. "A lot of people come into the league and get star-struck," he said, "and they can't do anything."

When I came out of the tunnel and looked up at that doughnut-shaped roof in Texas Stadium, I did feel a sense of awe. They tell you down there the little hole in the roof is so God can look down and see his favorite team play football. When you see it for the first time, you almost believe it.

The Dallas crowd got to you in those days, too—and not in the way you'd expect. The usual hometown crowd in the NFL will be noisy and rowdy. In Dallas, the crowd seemed sort of bored. It wasn't that they weren't into the game; they were. It was just that they had been accustomed to championship football for so long that they didn't get all that excited at ten-yard runs or fifteen-yard pass plays. They'd wait for their team to razzle-dazzle you for fifty, bomb you for seventy-five before they'd really holler. *That* was awesome.

For the most part, I didn't feel like a rookie, I felt like a ballplayer. In our first preseason game, at Soldier Field against the Bears, it wasn't the size of the crowd but the challenge of playing against guys like Walter Payton that turned me on. We won the game, 23–7. I had a whole bunch of tackles and a couple of sacks in the half I played. What I remember most is one play when Walter Payton came around my side, did this tiny little move that hung me in my jock, and went on up the field for twelve yards. I didn't leave the field in awe. I left in appreciation of one great player— and with an exact memory of that move so he couldn't pull it on me a second time.

Like any rookie, I remember my first regular-season game very well. I wasn't wide-eyed, I was just into the game—extra-hard. We played the Eagles at Giants Stadium. The year before they had gone to the Super Bowl and we hadn't beaten them since 1975 and were supposed to get our asses kicked again. We lost, 24–10, but it didn't quite feel that way. We played an intensely physical game. It might have been different.

I remember the game for two reasons. I got my first roughness call that afternoon. And I also hit Ron Jaworski so hard that I think he wound up being scared of me for the rest of his career. It all happened on the same play.

The first part of the play was simple: I bowled over this blocking back who was looking to keep me off his quarterback. In those days, teams hadn't yet adjusted their offenses to neutralize me—a blocking back on an outside linebacker was standard throughout the league.

Anyway, I knocked this guy on his ass and had a clear shot from the blind side at Jaworski. Now, one thing about me is I don't like to just wrap the quarterback, I really *try* to make him see seven fingers when they hold up three. I'll drive my helmet into him or, if I can, I'll bring my arm up over my head and try to ax the sonuvabitch in two. So long as the guy is holding that ball, I intend to hurt him. Not for the sake of hurting him but so he'll give up the football. Simple. Make him lose concentration. If I hit the guy right, I'll hit a nerve and he'll feel electrocuted, he'll forget for a few seconds that he's on a football field. I hit Jaworski that way— with an over-the-head ax job. I thought his dick was going to drop in the dirt. Then the refs dropped the flag on me.

I was pissed—there was nothing dirty about what I did; I don't need to be dirty. But you don't beat the zebras. Still, I knew I was okay because when I came to the sideline, Perk had this look in his eye. He told me, "I don't care if you get a hundred penalties like that, you just keep tackling that way." I did. Before the season was over, I hit a few other quarterbacks—and one of them, Neal Lomax of the Cardinals, wound up being permanently goofy against the Giants, along with Ron Jaworski.

The season before had been a losing one for the Giants, and no one was expecting us to do that much better in

1981—but we did. After losing three of our first five games, we put together a three-game winning streak, culminating with a big win in Atlanta. That Atlanta game probably was the turning point for us. Atlanta had gone to the playoffs the year before, and when we beat them, you could feel the excitement level rising among us.

The game started out badly for us. The Falcons got off to a 17–7 lead. It was cold and rainy and sloppy and you just knew it was going to be a miserable mud bath to the end. We got back in the game in the third period on a couple of touchdown passes, one to my roommate Dave.

Though Atlanta had put some points on the board, our defense was really playing well. We had a blocked punt for a TD, and we were making good, hard tackles throughout the game. We got sacks and fumble turnovers—I mean, we really got into this one—and it turned into a war.

We went ahead of Atlanta near the end of the game, but the Falcons came back to send it into overtime. On Atlanta's first possession after that, Brad creamed William Andrews, causing a fumble that we recovered and setting up our winning field goal, 27–24.

I remember this game because of another hit I had. This was the eighth week of the season, and by then teams were starting to do little things to stop me—nothing fancy, but enough to leave bruises and memories. I'd get a helmet in the chest, something in the ribs, a whole bunch of crack blocks. The game was still head-on, power-to-power—where I was going to win nearly all the time with my size and speed. But on this one play, near the end of regulation, Lynn Cain, a blocking back who most recently has been with the Rams, submarined me when I was coming toward the backfield.

It was like the guy was waiting to do it. I got there, he faked me one way and then went low, throwing me up in the air. In my mind, he was out to get me, not just stop me. I felt like I must have been up in the air twenty seconds before I came crashing back down to the ground. I was hurt—and I was pissed. I got to my feet and told the sonuvabitch he better watch his ass because I was going to get him. I did—on the very next play.

The Falcons ran this sweep to the other side, with Cain carrying the ball. He did a little spinning move and started to cut back to the inside—just as I was coming on like a pile-driver from behind. I hit him in the back of the head and I think I cracked a bone in his neck. They had to carry him off on a stretcher. I didn't care. If I believe someone has deliberately tried to injure me, they're going to get something back that will make them think.

Steve Streater had come down for the Atlanta game, so it was doubly sweet to win a big game and see him there. Because the team didn't go back to New York immediately afterward, we actually had some time to hang out.

I had a car take Steve back to the hotel where we were staying, and I was waiting for him out front when he arrived. I got him out of the car and into his chair and wheeled him straight through the hotel lobby to the bar, home territory.

We shot the shit same as ever.

There were a bunch of us together but all I could see was how cheerful and positive Steve was. We didn't spend time talking about heroism, injuries, or accidents. We just talked about old times, about the game, enjoying each other. He was looking good that day. He had been working out all along, getting ready for the day when he was going to walk again. I was glad that the season I had dedicated to him had a game in it like this one—which he just happened to be at.

We were a team that had obvious deficiencies but that had jelled and played well. We were loose and enjoyed each other a lot. I couldn't have cared less what had or hadn't happened in years past. All I know is that this team, on its way to the playoffs for the first time in ten years, got around to playing like a winning football team.

In our defensive huddle, no matter how tight things got,

there was a sense of fun. We'd start talking about cheer-leaders or where we'd go after the game. Then we'd go out and kick butt.

Because we were playing with a new 3–4 defensive alignment that year, even older players were having trouble keeping the play calls straight. I remember in one game, Brad walked up to me after we broke our huddle and said with this absolutely panicked look on his face:

"LT, where the fuck do I go on this play?"

I mean, I'm a rookie, it's the middle of a game, and here's Brad Van Pelt asking *me*, of all people, what to do.

"You've got to be kidding!" I said.

"It's no joke, man. *Am I supposed to cover, or what?*"

I started laughing my ass off. There was motion out to the flat and Brad was about to be hung.

"Good luck," I said. I must have sounded like Tonto telling the Lone Ranger to fend for himself at Custer's last stand.

But we were having a good time—on the field and off.

Away from the field, life got to be brighter and faster than ever. Brad and Brian had years of experience in the NFL and just as many tasting the Big Apple to the core. These guys knew places in New York City Kojak never dreamed about. One time, a couple of my boys had come up from Virginia to hang out with me, and one night we all hit the city with Brad and Brian.

Sometime in the early hours we went to this brownstone in the eighties—I've been looking for it ever since. Brad rang the bell downstairs and soon this peephole shot open and then a door was opened for us. I was drunk but I was telling myself, "Uh-oh, what are we in for now?"

We went up some stairs, through another door, and then were in this brightly lit room that had a bar, all kinds of gambling tables, roulette wheels, and blackjack tables. There were people in gorgeous clothes and dancing and music.

I bought a couple of hundred dollars' worth of chips, went over to the blackjack table, and put down the whole stack for my first hand. I was told I couldn't do that; the limit was $100. I left a hundred out there, got an ace and a nine, and then doubled down to get another card—remember, I had had a few. I pulled another ace—to get 21! I could see people—including the folks who ran the place—giving me all kinds of looks. Fuck it, play the cards!

D'Fellas suddenly started harmonizing in the middle of all this. Brad and Brian couldn't believe it. I kept on winning. D'Fellas kept on singing. I get a feel for how I'm going to do in cards with my first hand of the evening—and I sure had gotten the feeling then. I won eleven, twelve hundred dollars just like that. Then I got up from the table and said, "That's it."

You don't do that to people who are having their pockets cleaned. Oh, no!

There were all kinds of smooth, mean-looking types who suddenly slid up to me wanting to know if I wouldn't like to stay and have some drinks, enjoy some music.

I told these people, sure—it was just that we'd forgotten something outside and would be right back. We got out of there in the nick of time.

On the field, the first winning season the Giants had had in ten years made everyone's life happy. I think in the entire time I've been with the Giants—including Super Bowl XXI—this kind of closeness was never matched. We were not greatly skilled and we were not all crazies, but as professionals we were as close to being a family as teams get. Guys I didn't hang out with, guys like George Martin, became a part of this experience as much as other guys I did hang out with. George was straight as an arrow, a man of God, a player who used the skills he had. He wasn't overly big, wasn't a great pass rusher or tackler—but he used all his skills to the fullest advantage: the opposite of someone like me, maybe. But around him, I felt this aura of respect and admiration. You felt privileged just to know him and to play alongside him. He was—and is, to this day—an inspiration.

People weren't looking for us to make it to the playoffs, but we did. We had to beat Dallas at home in the last game of the season and then get help from the Jets, who were playing the Packers the following day, to make it.

The game against the Cowboys took place on a gray, windy, snowy day—this was the other time in my life I played football in the snow—but you could feel the electricity in the crowd and in our locker room. For the older players and the younger ones—maybe for different reasons—this one was so special.

I didn't think we'd make it for a while. We were down, 10–3, late in the game and needed a big fourth-down reception by John Mistler from Scott Brunner to keep us going. Both these guys—Brunner, particularly—had been there for us in our drive for the playoffs. Brunner took over at quarterback in the Washington game five weeks earlier when Phil Simms went out for the year with a shoulder separation. And Scott came in and did a job. Mistler wasn't a factor that much in games, but the guy had great hands and caught everything that came his way in practice, so it was no surprise to see him there now, when it counted. We hit a tying field goal into the wind with thirty seconds left to take the game into overtime.

In the extra session, I thought we had it won when I creamed Tony Dorsett deep in Dallas territory, causing a fumble and turnover. I came off the field so happy I was crying. But a chip-shot field-goal try hit the crossbar and it wasn't over yet.

My roommate Byron intercepted Danny White to set up another chip shot—which Joe Danelo hit this time—before we finally won. You couldn't believe the scene on that field unless maybe you had been a longtime Giant fan or veteran player.

I was excited and happy, of course. Byron and I a few other guys went out and partied our asses off afterward, but the older guys were happy in ways I could never be. Brad came up to me on the field right afterward and started hugging me, jumping up and down. "Thank you! Thank you! Thank you!" he kept saying. It was beautiful—but it was strange. As happy as I was, I wound up feeling a little like a spectator. I had always played with winning teams and didn't know what losing really was.

We all went back to the stadium the next day to watch the Jets and Green Bay on TV. When the Jets won, these older guys just went crazy again. There was champagne everywhere and they were crying—it was a sight to see—and all the while I was standing there thinking, "It's not *that* big a deal." We still had some unfinished business out there.

When we beat Philadelphia in the wild-card game the following week, that might not have been as exciting—but it meant plenty to us. People had said we backed into the playoffs. But when we won this game—against a team that had been NFC champs the year before—the Giants had respect. We were no fluke. Even some of the guys on our team who might have begun the year not expecting much could now see we were better than people gave us credit for. We might have been short on ability, but the lunch-pail Giants were born in that season.

We were knocked out in the semis by San Francisco, 38–24. We were beaten by a better team, but it was a good game to be in—we made them fight for everything they got— and it hurt like hell to lose. I came out of that game angry, steaming, not wanting to talk to anyone, especially the press. My troubles with the media probably began with this game—years before they started looking for other reasons. I told Vinnie, our clubhouse man, to keep the press away, but they came after me anyway. I went off on them, tattooed them to the point where there were headlines and stories the following day about my having to learn that losing was part of football. What else is new?

I made my amends later on, but I'll be damned if I ever will take losing differently. When I lose, I have feelings about it. Period. It isn't the writers who are down on the field losing, it's us. You want it differently? Suit up, go out, get your ass kicked, and see how it feels.

That game was important for me in another way. The 49ers were the first team in the NFL to use an interior lineman to block me. They used John Ayers, a 6-5, 265-pound guard and had him pulling all day. The sonuvabitch was in my face constantly, and I couldn't figure out what to do with him.

Word obviously got around the league fast.

I was never again allowed to play battering ram with tight ends and blocking backs.

Too bad. It was fun while it lasted.

12

I couldn't have had a better rookie year. I was Rookie of the Year, Defensive Lineman of the Year, was named—unanimously—to the Pro Bowl. There have been ten times—including 1987—when a player went to the Pro Bowl on a unanimous vote of his fellow players and coaches; six of those ten times it was me.

Of course I was happy, but the thing about any award is that it is for the moment. It's really about the past, not the future. When I finally quit football, I will have had about ten years in the league—and after that, all the rings, all the glory, all the awards will have passed.

Things that are personal stay with you, goals you set for yourself—like getting to the Super Bowl, the closeness of your family and the people you love, how well you actually play when you go out there from game to game—these will always remind you more about who you are and what you've done than awards and trophies.

In my first year I just wanted to play. I remember being at the Front Row, a bar near Giants Stadium, after a game and this guy came up to me and said that he'd been watching players come and go for years and that I was going to sweep every award in sight. I turned the guy off; I didn't want to listen to him. Don't get me wrong. When I got to Hawaii that

Waiting to go—versus the Washington Redskins. *Photo © Fred Roe*

Harry Carson and I at the Pro Bowl in 1985. I've gone to the Pro Bowl every year since I joined the NFL—but because of seniority, my number, 56, regularly goes to Doug Smith of the Rams. *Photo © Chris Schwenk*

Bill has always been a player's coach. I've argued with him sometimes and benefited from him always. Bill was there when I needed him most— when I had my problem. *Photo © Fred Roe*

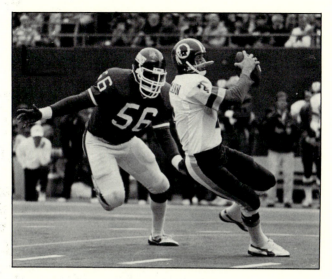

In this shot, from October 1985, I'm about to hit Joe
Theisman. It's amazing how life repeats itself. A month
later, a hit just like this one—on national television—
ended Joe's career. It is not a moment I want to remember—
or see again. *Photo © Fred Roe*

Formation "Fire-Lion-Zero-Down"—just one element of the terrific
Giants defensive system. I am keyed on Redskins running back Kelvin
Bryant in the 1987 NFC title game. We completely closed down the
Skins running game and won, 17–0. *Photo © Fred Roe*

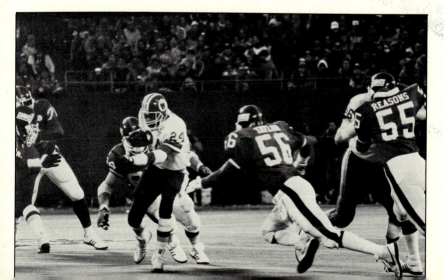

Two of the toughest men you'll find on the New York Giants. Lamar Leachman, our defensive line coach, taught me some of the nastiest moves I know. *Photo © Fred Roe*

Win or lose, the Giant defensive unit has always played with pride. Even when you lose, you play for pride in your unit. *Photo © Fred Roe*

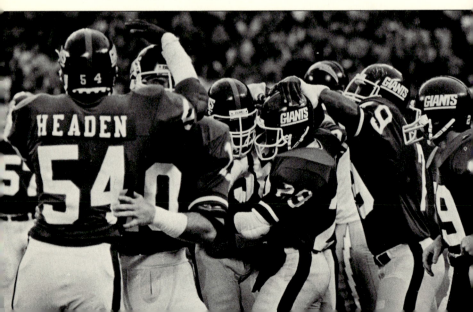

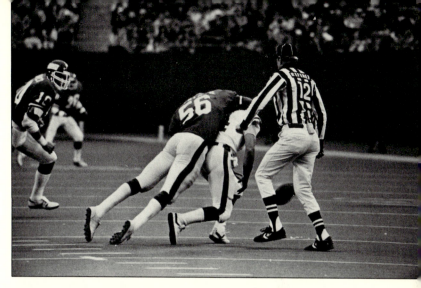

There are sacks and there are *sacks*. This is a *sack*. Richard
Todd of the New York Jets is losing the football and maybe
some feeling in his neck and shoulders. You don't want to
injure a guy, just make him hurt enough to drop the ball.
Photo © Fred Roe

Lowering the boom on Gary Hogeboom of the Dallas
Cowboys. *Photo © Fred Roe*

There was sheer joy in taking the '49ers apart 49–3 in the 1986 playoffs. *Photo © Fred Roe*

The D does a dance after George Martin sacks John Elway in the second quarter of Super Bowl XXI. The game turned into a rout, but this was a key play at the time. *AP/Wide World Photos*

Phil Simms and I sharing a moment after winning the Super Bowl. Phil put the doubters to rest forever at Pasadena. No quarterback ever had a better game—unless it was on another planet. *AP/ Wide World Photos*

I was only the second defensive player ever to win the NFL Most Valuable Player of the Year award, and the first to win the Schick Player of the Year award. I was happy and grateful to win some big awards last season, but some of it came from surprise over my "comeback," I'm sure. *Photo © Dan Miller*

What's ahead? I have two playing years left on my contract
and that should be it. I want to go out while I'm on top.
Photo © Fred Roe

year and I was walking around on the beach at the time of the Pro Bowl, it finally hit me: I really had myself a season.

But where this counted most was when I went home and could share some of it with my mom and pop, my friends and old schoolteachers, all the folks who knew me growing up—and who I would never have to be "different" for.

I went on up to North Carolina to be with Linda and my son, T.J., who had been born the past August. We still weren't married—there were still all kinds of people telling me that it was crazy to be married and also play in the NFL—but there was no way I wasn't going to marry Linda.

Steve, whom I had dedicated my first season to, was also in Chapel Hill. My "award" there was that I could spend time with him, just as we always had. I remember going to his apartment along with a few other players who had come back to town for a visit—Donnell Thompson and some other old teammates—and we went on uptown like it was any other Saturday night.

We went to Purdy's, one of those joints off Franklin Street, and we all carried Steve up a flight of stairs in his chair. We drank, clowned around—just as we always had—and there were a couple of belligerent assholes from Duke—just as there used to be.

"Hit 'em, Taylor, kick their ass!" Steve hollered.

I didn't. But if I had, I'm pretty sure Steve would have turned his chair right into the middle of things.

The year was over and it was the future, not the past, I had to deal with. Not all the awards or personal rewards guarantee one second of the future. No one ever knows what's around the next bend in the road—and when it comes to a guy like me, that is almost a literal statement. It turns out that I got to my next year—and all the ones after that—lucky to be alive.

The Giants don't know this—I don't think anybody

does other than the people immediately involved, my friend Paul Davis, Linda and her family, a few local cops, and a doctor—but I was nearly killed in a car crash while I was down in Carolina.

I had been at some banquet with Paul and we were coming back late at night. We had had a few, and there were a couple of six-packs alongside us in the car, though neither of us were anywhere near ripped. It was early March and the weather was cold for Carolina. There had been some snow and rain recently. We were going at a pretty good clip when all of a sudden we hit a patch of ice.

I thought that was it. But then the car came out of it. Even before I had a chance to say "Oh, shit!" we hit another patch of ice going around a curve. And this time the car didn't straighten out. We saw lights coming toward us and we just started spinning crazily across the road. It couldn't have been more than a second or two but then we hit a ravine and flipped over, slamming into a tree. I remember hearing this terrific sound—BAM!—and then seeing trees pushed up against the door next to me.

I probably could have been more sober than I was because I remember saying to Paul, "Damn, I've got to drive this car home like this—I just know this bad boy got a big ole dent in it."

Davis had gotten out of the car and was standing there shaking his head. He said, "This car ain't goin' nowhere home, boy, this sonuvabitch is wrapped around a tree."

When I think back on it now, crazy as it is to say it, I think if I *hadn't* been physically relaxed I would have been dead. The whole front part of the car was shoved up against my chest. The foot pedals were all bent and mangled. And, I then found out, I couldn't move.

Paul pulled me out of the car and lay me down on the grass. I realized I still couldn't move. I was lying on the grass and it was snowing and I was suddenly scared.

"Paul," I said, "the beer, the beer!"

He thought I was delirious.

"Get the beer out of the car and get rid of it before the cops come." All I could think of was that when the cops came they'd find alcohol in the car, and the Giants and everybody else would know about it in the next morning's newspapers.

Davis did get rid of the beer, and when the cops arrived a short while later, I still could barely move. They were going to call an ambulance for me, but the idea of going to the hospital scared me as much as the idea of the cops finding booze in the car—for just the same reasons. I hurt like a sonuvabitch but I wasn't paralyzed.

I told the cops not to bother, that I was really just shaken up, that more than anything I wanted to go home. The cops drove me on to Linda's house, where I had a private doctor come in to see me. It turned out I had a severe bruise of the sternum, some badly banged-up ribs—and nothing broken.

A word here about Mr. Davis from Appalachia, Virginia. Paul was my last roommate in college and over the years he has become an honorary Fella. He got drafted and cut by the Raiders the same year I went to the Giants. Three years and two teams later, he was out of football. He's had a tough life. But he's been my friend from day one because he's been 100 percent loyal and 100 percent straight with me. To this day I can count on him—for better or worse—to cut right through the bullshit every time.

Though the Giants never found out about this particular incident, I don't think they were in the dark about me in any other way.

One day a couple of years later, our trainer, Ronnie Barnes, was working on me and very casually let me know that George Young, the Giants' general manager, had told him that he didn't expect me to live past the age of thirty. I was the Troy Archer type, he said. Archer, a first-round Giants defensive tackle in 1976, was killed in a truck accident in 1979. George, Ronnie Barnes said, had taken out a $2 million life insurance policy on me.

My attitude then—and now—was, So what? I have no idea if I'll make it to thirty. I want to, I'm surely not looking to kill myself—or anyone else. A friend of mine recently asked about my driving habits. I told him I didn't wear seat belts because if I ever got in a crash at the speed I go, I wouldn't survive anyway. I told him the truth: that I knew all about the dangers drinking and driving brought other people. But I also told him what I tell anyone else who asks: If I don't care what happens to me now, can I really think about what might happen to others? I don't think of myself as a bad driver—I feel safer behind the wheel than any time I'm in a passenger seat—but if I were George Young I'd probably do just what he did.

There were a few other surprises waiting for me my next season. In preseason, I injured my foot. Injuries can happen at any time to you in football. You can be the biggest star in the game one day and out of it the next. I happened to get a relatively minor injury, something called turf toe—it's like a bone bruise or a small break. It is a nagging injury and it slows you down. I was slowed when the season started, and my injury didn't seem to improve with time.

There was another unexpected cloud on the horizon. Only a speck in the sky the season before, a players' strike blew up into a real storm in my second season. We were playing Green Bay in the second game of the year—at home—and everybody, by then, knew that a strike was at hand. The Green Bay game was to be our last before what we all thought would be a strike of several days or a week.

It was a Monday night game and nobody was really into it. The only reason I remember that it was even a Monday night game was because, twice, the lights in Giants Stadium went out. It was weird: It was like we weren't supposed to be there. We stood around, all of us, not knowing what to do, not really being in the game anyway, half of us sure that the blackouts were related to the strike. Whatever, there were forces beyond our control. The next morning I was out of a job—along with every other player in the league.

Linda and I had finally gotten married. We were in the process of building a house and now, suddenly, with the money I had spent for my parents' house, the cutoff in income from the strike was something I had just never counted on. We were living in a hotel, waiting to move, but then came this business of a strike.

I didn't feel concerned right away because I really did assume things would be cleaned up pretty quickly. There were a number of other players living in the hotel with us, and for a few days all of us would meet, shoot the shit, and hold informal workouts. We were all looking to go back to work.

But the strike went on for eight weeks—from the end of September to almost the end of November—and pretty soon, instead of playing out my second season, as I had expected, I found myself, with my new family, out of a house and a hotel, on the road between New York, Carolina, and my folks' place in Virginia. For a while things were scrambled but not bad. I had a chance to go back and see my old high school team play a game. They brought me out onto the field at halftime and there was a little ceremony for me—and in the time I was down there I had a chance to visit at school and get together with D'Fellas. I saw a game at North Carolina, too, and spent time with old friends there.

But finally, all these weeks when I should have been playing football for the Giants got to weigh a lot. I played tons of golf, drank a whole lot, and hung around feeling nastier and nastier—the strike delay was no highlight for me. I wound up making life sorry for Linda.

I have to say, the issues of the strike never grabbed me, either. I'm enough of a union person to know that you win and lose as a team, but I thought the issue of revenue sharing—which we went out for—was mainly bullshit. I think the union went for a big attack because in the past it had made a lot of mistakes. But the big attack, in this case, wasn't directed where it should have been.

Suppose the issue of profit sharing had been accepted. That would have definitely benefited marginal players, but it wouldn't have helped exceptional players. If we had won, I would never have been able to negotiate another contract; everything would have been structured. Why would an owner even think of negotiating anything with a player when he's got a structure controlling things? Under the formula that had been talked about, a marginal player who had been in the league the same number of years but who didn't play as much or as well as an outstanding player would make the same amount of money. I didn't buy that.

The union *does* have issues to fight for—free agency, for example—that will benefit all players. Free agency raises salaries. It's done that in baseball—even though the owners are trying to reverse it now—and it's done it with basketball.

I happen to like the union leadership. I like Gene Upshaw, think he has a good head on his shoulders, and I liked Ed Garvey. But the union has been in existence for six years and I can't really see what's been accomplished that's justified yearly dues increasing from $300 to $1,500. It's true that the '82 strike effort would have—and did—benefit players who needed help. Players with injuries or who had grievances got something. But even there, because the issues weren't really correct, marginal players suffered, too. They weren't protected at all when the contract had escalating salaries for them with a big jump in the fourth year. That meant that if you were a reserve in the NFL, the chances were great that you would be cut—and a first-year player hired—after you reached your fourth year in the league. Try that on for size if your game is special teams.

I would have been happy to strike for a real issue, but not for bullshit.

There were a couple of other surprises waiting out there for me in '82. One was that when the strike ended, I wound up, after one game, sitting on the bench. That was Bill's choice because, he said, my injury still had not healed. He thought I had been slow in practices and that it showed up in the Washington game that first week back.

I didn't agree. My toe still hurt like a sonuvadog, but I'll be damned if I wanted to sit. I got into it with Bill pretty heavily. I mean, I knew I was well enough to play and help the team; and I also, personally, believe that the only time you sit with an injury is when you can't walk. I had a concussion during a game in '84. When I was standing on the sidelines in a fog, I grabbed my helmet and yelled to the bench, "If I do bad things out there, take me out!" I ran back out onto the field. I wasn't trying to prove anything, I just don't want to sit—ever.

When I finally got into that '82 game—it was against Detroit—it turned out that what I did on the field made the only argument that carried any weight with Bill: I could play. We won the game, 13–6, on a 97-yard pass interception I made in the fourth quarter. The Lions had a third down on our four-yard line: They could have run, they could have passed. I could tell from the way they split their backs that they might just have one of them coming out of the backfield as a receiver. Horace King came out right at me. I knew where the guy's cut was before their quarterback even threw the ball. I caught the ball directly in front of him and I was off.

I ran—and ran and ran. They say that Bill was over there on the sidelines at the fifty screaming, "Run! Run! Run!" as I passed him, but I didn't hear him. I was worried about getting hauled down from behind. Each time I turned, I got a quick look at someone running stride for stride with me. At the Detroit twenty, I had one more look and realized it was my own shadow. That was something! But the big thing for me then was worrying about what to do when I hit the end zone. I didn't want to slam the ball down or do some stupid dance—my mind just went blank on me. All I could think of was that baseball had been my first love when I was a kid. I did a hook slide into the end zone.

There was one more surprise—a big one—in '82. Two games before the end of the season, Perk shocked everybody on the team by resigning, and Bill was named his successor.

I'm not sure why Perk left any more than anyone else. He had his problems with some guys on the team—every coach does—but if there was something going on there that made him want to quit, I don't know what it was. I know that he was fair to me—despite what some people have said— and I know what he felt about winning. I don't think I've ever met a coach who was as intense about winning as Ray Perkins. You could see it in his eyes. I mean, the man didn't need words when he came after you; if he looked at you with those eyes of his he could freeze you into stone. Maybe he left because he saw hard and troubled times coming. Maybe it was just as he said, because he wanted to go home. I do know that I was sorry to see him go. Just as I was glad to see Bill named head coach.

Bill was as different from Perk as night from day. Bill was more easygoing, more accessible to the players—a "players' coach" in that he had loyalties to the guys that sometimes made it hard for him to make decisions on who should sit and who should play. Later on, I believe that got in his way, because believe me, the only thing in this game is winning. But at that point it was like having one of the guys become head coach.

I don't think of 1982 as a great year. I wound up in the Pro Bowl again and was Defensive Player of the Year for the second straight time, but there was no way it was as much fun or was as exciting as my first year. We didn't make the playoffs; we finished with a losing record and lost half our games to the strike.

I suppose you could say 1982 was a year of surprises, but except for another little cloud on the horizon, 1982 would also have been a forgettable year for me.

1982 just happened to be the season when I first began using drugs.

13

I used drugs only occasionally and always recreationally before it became a "problem" in 1985. I used them at first because they were available. I didn't need them, they didn't affect the way I played football in any way, and when I did use them, I enjoyed them—there was never any reason to pay much attention to what was, after all, only partying back then. Hell, I could handle partying. I was the guy who could walk up the sides of buildings blind drunk in the middle of the night. If I had a problem it was out there on the football field.

The 1983 season was the beginning of the Bill Parcells era, and it sure didn't look like a Super Bowl would ever be part of it. It's only been in the last year that we moved out and became a dominant team in the league; you never would have seen it coming that year. We were a losing team, and it seemed for a while that losing, not anything else, was the real addiction.

We went 3–12–1 in 1983 and along the way found ways to lose games that even were more surprising to us than to the fans. We gave games away on interceptions, fumbles, missed field goals, dropped punts, you name it. I frankly couldn't believe what I saw out there. It was like nothing I had ever experienced on a football field.

When the season began, I fully expected us to do well. I

had seen Scott Brunner the year we went to the playoffs, and from the four or five games he played, I knew he could move the ball. He had been like a breath of fresh air. He made mistakes, but he made more plays than mistakes. In a year's time, through all of 1983, he was perhaps the worst quarterback I've ever seen. It was just impossible to believe. The guy threw interception after interception, took sack after sack, played giveaway time and time again. I can't begin to figure out what happened to him. Maybe he had personal problems, maybe he took too many shots to the head or lost his confidence. Whatever, in a year's time he turned into Donald Duck in a football suit.

It didn't help when we went to other quarterbacks, either. Phil Simms got healthy long enough to get his thumb broken in the fifth game of the season—he was out for the year again. And when Jeff Rutledge took over a couple of games later, he lasted only until the following week, when he threw a whole bunch of interceptions and got his knee mangled in the process. We didn't see Jeff again until the last two games of the season. We went to the bottom with Scott Brunner.

A lot more than a losing season was involved. When you play on a losing team, things happen to you. You subtly start to change your ways of thinking.

What I had always thought was that football was about winning. There was no reason to play the game other than to win. You're fed bullshit about playing well, but only winning counts. If you lose, you're not around long. Losing is contagious. If you lose too much, you wind up losing off the field, too. Why, I don't know—but it happens.

On the Giants, the only defense we had against losing was the defense. It became a defense in defense of ourselves. The defensive unit on the Giants had always been strong, from the days of Y. A. Tittle and Sam Huff. It was a Giant tradition when I arrived, and it will be one when I leave. And in that losing year—and afterward—the defense made it possible to go out there and play with pride. In spite of the year we had, we still wound up with the third-best defense in the NFL. We were first in allowing fewest third-down conversions, and we were right there in nearly all the other statistical categories.

But what happens on a losing team is that you look for pride not on the team as a whole but in different parts of the team. You look to the unit you play in, and if that doesn't work, you look to personal pride. Because we had such a good defense, we became even tighter as a unit—on and off the field.

On the field, we took the attitude that the offense didn't even exist. No one criticized the offensive players, but we all knew that our best chance of winning was by keeping the offense *off* the field as much as possible. Not only did we keep ourselves in games when we were out there, we also had a better chance of putting points on the board. Our motto was simple: Keep the offense on the bench and give us a chance to win.

The more we knew we were a losing team, the more the team broke down into these smaller units. This breakdown occurs anyway. Receivers, quarterbacks, linemen, linebackers, defensive backs, etc.—all are little teams within the team, and all have their own characters.

The linebacking corps, then as now, was the heart of the team. It is hard to describe what playing alongside guys like Harry, Brad, and Brian was like. In some way, playing with these guys was like getting on-the-job training. They were coaches as much as they were players. Brian in particular was a kind of father figure to all the linebackers. He was so smart out there, I can still hear him yelling to the coordinators on the sidelines in the middle of a game, "No, you mean this!" or "What about doing it this way?"—and they'd shake their heads and say, "Right! Right!"

Harry was another kind of father figure. Because he was an older player and had given so much to the team, he commanded respect from just about everyone. But he had other sides as well. The fans saw a very intense, very articulate, very accommodating personality. He was that. But that wasn't all of Harry. There was Harry and his women. I shared a locker next to him, and I mean the man got tons of letters from admiring women every day. I never saw anything like it. For sure, Harry didn't know one one-thousandth of these women who were pouring their hearts out to him in these letters. I mean, he would read them to me as much amazed as I was.

I learned over the years that Harry Carson is really a very complicated person, and I'm not sure I understand him to this day. He is the kind of guy who calls team meetings endlessly because he wants us to rally together. I know how much it hurts him to lose. And I know what kind of a football player he is. But he also is a man who, for reasons best known to him, will carry things too far. He'll say things about you in public, among your teammates and coaches, that you might laugh off in private but that hurt you when it's out there in the street. Harry is the kind of guy who'll stand up for you then try to put you down. He'll carry on almost like a college professor in meetings till you want to go to sleep, then he'll turn around and start saying and doing things that you wouldn't expect from a college freshman.

When I think of Brad, I think of him along with Brian and of the good times we all had together. All of those practices when we linebackers would leave the stadium and say, almost together, "Where are we going?" Because we enjoyed each other tremendously. But I also think of Brad in terms of what losing did to him. The teams he had been on had lost for so long that I think it must have changed him. I think somewhere along the line he got used to losing, told himself it was all right so long as he just played well, which he always did. But I believe he wound up coming to the stadium no longer expecting to win. He had years on him when he left, but what he really had on him was too much losing.

Losing did things to me, too. In this game, when the team isn't working, you better make sure you are. You cover your own ass—that is a fundamental law of survival in the NFL. I had a lot to learn as a ballplayer. I hadn't gotten accustomed to losing by any means, but it allowed me to look harder at what I did—technically—on a football field.

If you're only somewhat into football, it may look like most of what I do out there now is pure power. My game, by this third year, had increasingly become mental and technical. I worked hard to become a better football player.

Starting from the end of my first year, when I began to face interior linemen as blockers, I had to make adjustments. And to tell you the truth, if I hadn't been forced to change that, I probably would have been wheeled off the field on a meat cart. My body at the end of one year hurt from head to toe.

It wasn't easy for me to adjust because I believe the strength of my game absolutely depends—to this day—on instinct. Resorting to technique, no matter what your coaches say, risks losing that split second or two when you either get to a play or see it go by you. But by 1983, when the playbook had finally become familiar and when I had had enough games under my belt, I could do it. Playing alongside the kinds of teammates I had helped—and so did Bill Parcells and Lamar Leachman, our defensive line coach, who worked with me to develop some new moves.

Taking care of pulling guards—which I first ran into in that Frisco playoff game in '81—turned out to be relatively simple. Most big guards, like John Ayers of the 49ers, just want to hit you and drive you outside. If you hit the guard as hard as you can, stopping his momentum, then work his hands—knock them up or down or anywhere so he can't get them on you—you can slip him. Or if you work with another lineman—a Leonard Marshall or a Casey Merrill—you would hit the offensive tackle in the ribs, kick him inside so your teammate can go around you, like you were picking for him in basketball. You'd have the guard right in your face, but your teammate would slip to the outside for a clear, unopposed rush. That might force teams to adjust their plans for you.

When teams started dropping tackles on me or using combinations of tackles, tight ends, and backs—they did it all the time by '83—that demanded a lot more. Tackles, unlike backs or even pulling guards, don't depend on the force of their forward momentum to stop you. They drop back to *absorb* your rush. A big tackle dropping back three or four yards and fanning out is the hardest of all to contend with.

Double teams are something else. Normally you would think they make life tougher for you. Sometimes they do, sometimes they don't. A double team means—right away—that another player is freed up. A double team also can give you a kind of psychological edge. Let's say you're going to get double-teamed by a lineman and a back. One of the guys, unconsciously, because he sees the other trying to beat the shit out of you, is going to let up ever so slightly. He won't mean to, but he will. If you shed the lineman fast—say, by using a technical thing like a double slap with an upper cut—you'll get past the lineman and be at the back with momentum enough to slam the sonuvabitch or turn right past him.

By the third year, I started working with the full range of six or seven moves I regularly use now to free myself from blockers. I started paying more attention to the adjustments and counteradjustments, to the mental side of what I was doing. For example, I learned to conserve my moves, maybe using only one or two of them in a game. Today I wait to see who the quarterback is and what he's doing. If he's someone like Joe Montana or Dan Fouts—someone with a short drop and a quick release—I won't waste moves to get at him, because I won't be able to. Any move I use in one game will be on our next opponent's game films.

In the past, I used to make it a point of not knowing

much about who I was playing against. I didn't want to know because I felt it was better left to instinct, which would always lead me to quicker reaction time—and reaction time was everything. Well, when offenses started gearing for me, they'd do all kinds of things to throw me off. Knocking me on my ass was the least of it. Smart teams like Dallas and Washington and Seattle would run all kinds of false keys and misdirections to get me to commit myself. They'd get me to react rather than simply to act. They'd run a draw where you almost had to read pass, or they'd do the reverse. They'd throw pulling linemen at you, getting you to look for a run one way, and then they'd go the other.

So the mental part for me became a way of reading and responding technically. I started thinking about situations much more. On third-down or long-yardage situations, I'd go strictly off instinct; that was a sack down. But on first- or second-down situations it was where you were and who was running against you. You needed to know things. When you ran against a tackle like, say, J. T. Smith of the Cardinals, you needed to know that he usually set short and inside and that the most effective technique against him would be a slap, spin, second slap, and power rush.

I've always had a sharp visual sense of the field. Basketball players like Magic Johnson and Larry Bird have that. Everything, excluding the wide out to my blind side, I see all at once. It's as if I can watch many players all doing their different things as a single body. Nature gave me that. But I was learning now to do other things. When a lineman sets, is he ever so slightly forward on his feet, or is he back on his heels? Right off, that tells you if he's blocking for a run or for pass protection. Sometimes linemen are skillful enough not to tip things that way. You watch the fingers of their set. Sometimes—especially with white linemen—you'll be able to see their fingernails go all white. If they do, it means the pressure of their weight is forward—it's going to be a run.

Now, if it's going to be a run, what kind of run is it going to be? I knew by my second year that most teams ran away from me, not at me. I happen to *hate* being shut out of a play. If you stop me from running, you go a long way toward taking the fun of the game away from me. If the fun goes out of playing on any given day, I'm halfway to being beaten.

Good pursuit, which I've always been known for, isn't automatic when your opposition is as good as you regularly find in the pros. When a team sets up to run to the strong side and I'm camped over there on the weak side, there's a problem of *how* you get over to the other side in time to make a play. Of course speed is essential. But I learned that I couldn't count on my speed alone. I had to learn the angles of pursuit I was using.

Say a guy runs a sweep to the left, you're on the right. If you just trail after the guy's ass, you won't catch him unless he's slow. Over the years—from the time I first came into the league till now—most teams have gone to a one-back offense, and the one back is usually a speedy running back rather than a slower fullback. What I learned to do was to come at him from a different angle. I couldn't cut across the field in front of the line of scrimmage, the most direct line to cutting him off; there were too many bodies in the way. But I found that if I started a step or two into the backfield, then cut sharply behind and parallel to the line of scrimmage, I very often could get an unobstructed lane across the field. Give me that and I have a chance to hang a nasty surprise on a runner.

When I look back now, I know why 1983 was for me such a good year. I not only played well, I also played somewhat differently—I became a better, smarter player in that year. For a while during the season, when Harry was injured for a few games, I was moved over to his position: inside linebacker. I hated it. On the inside there's just too much in the way, too many bodies, too many obstructed views, too little that instinct alone can take advantage of. But for the time I was there, I probably was helped—just because I had so many adjustments to make.

I wound up playing for personal pride in 1983, which turned out to be another Pro Bowl year. But I also knew that personal accomplishments were no substitutes for winning. When losing becomes a habit, when you drop back into playing for no more than personal pride, you wind up saying, whether you intend to or not, to hell with the rest.

I never was and never will be that kind of football player.

Learning is great, but I'd rather be dumb and win any day.

14

ME and systems. I think if I had come along in the sixties, I would have been antinuke, antiwar, anti- just about everything worth protesting. Probably would have wound up one dead black man. If I see something I don't like or think is wrong or something that just catches my fancy, I'll do something about it. Sometimes I'll do it because I'm pissed off, sometimes because I just feel like having a good time, other times because it just makes sense.

One day, before I cleared out of Carolina, for instance, I got asked to visit a dying kid at the Duke University Burn Center. The kid was a high school player who admired me or something, so I went to see him. He had third-degree burns and was so sick he had stopped eating—the surest sign, the doctors said, that he was going to die. It turned out the kid wasn't eating because he hated hospital food and the rules said he couldn't have food from the outside. Fuck that. I went out, bought a steak, snuck it back in, and shared it with him. If that kid was dying, it was from the rules, not from his burns. He ate like a horse. (P.S.: He's fine today.)

On the military style of a football team, particularly a losing one, that sort of attitude can make the ball take a few funny bounces.

By end of '82 and right to the present, my feeling about rules and regulations was no different than it had been when

I played football in Carolina. I'm going to do what I want. It's as simple as that. If someone doesn't like it, fine; if someone wants to join the ranks of the renegades with me, that's fine, too. The rule in both cases is the same: You better play as well as I do because it won't mean anything otherwise.

Now, the Giants, like most other professional teams, put out a list of things you will be fined for if you don't stay in line. Reading them over, you can get to feel that management has this preconceived notion that they are dealing with a bunch of bad Cub Scouts. There are about thirty punishable infractions in the club rules. You get hit five bucks if you forget to pay your hotel bill, twenty-five for being overweight (per pound per day), a hundred bucks for being late to a weigh-in, team promotional activity, meeting, doctor's appointment, or bed check, or for playing your stereo too loud or for chucking a football into the stands. You get nailed five hundred for missing a weigh-in, meeting, promotional activity, appointment, etc. It's a thousand bucks each day of training camp missed. And if you have a gun or a woman in your room, watch out: That's a whole week's pay and a possible suspension. (I haven't yet been able to figure out why the folks who run things believe women and guns are equal threats.)

I think I've been fined sixty, seventy, eighty thousand bucks since I've joined the Giants. I've never bothered to count, and frankly I couldn't care less. I never liked the idea of hiding. One time Casey Merrill and I stuck a couple of inflated dolls we bought at a sex shop into our beds before we snuck off for the night. Trial and error. I did it, but it wasn't my style. I felt like a bad Cub Scout.

Another time, during training camp, I went through this elaborate escape from the dormitory after curfew. I went out a window, across a ledge, through another window, down to a basement, and out a side door that led to a path that took me up into the woods. I was going through these woods when I noticed a figure coming toward me. I wasn't paying much attention and it was too dark to see anyway. It turned out this was one of the coaches, Johnny Parker. As he passed, he said, "Hello, Lawrence." When I realized who it was, I turned back and caught up with him.

"Hey, Coach, you're not going to turn me in, are you?" I asked.

"You know I have to."

I went back to the dorm with him and on to my room. A couple of the guys saw me come in and asked me why I had come back so soon. I told them what had happened. They laughed.

"You've already lost the fine. Why did you need to come back?"

Hey, right! I turned around, went on back downstairs, through the lobby where a number of the coaches were sitting—I said hello to them—and went out the front door. I've done everything by the front door ever since.

Beginning in 1983, things got a little more serious. Maybe it had to do with too much losing, maybe it was just an ongoing sense that game day always mattered far more to me than the rest of the week, but I wound up taking the same attitudes toward practice that I had toward the rules in general. If you knew what you had to do out there on Sunday, the rest of it was just something you had to go through. Long before the media started writing about my going to sleep in meetings—proof, they said, that I was drug-impaired—I started dozing during long film sessions. Or asking the coach to rerun an especially crazy-looking hit—if you don't want films to bore you to death, you try to turn them into cartoons.

I also took liberties when I wanted to at practice. At the end of our practice sessions, we are always asked to do laps. Some teams make you do them within a specific time; the Giants didn't. You just had to do them. Well, sometimes I didn't even do that. The coaches would get everybody off running, and I'd walk into the locker room with them. If they fined me, so be it. I didn't like running in high school, I still don't like it today—unless it ends with a running back or a quarterback sticking out of the ground.

I started showing up late for practice, too. And once I didn't show up at all. That day I got a call at home at one o'clock in the afternoon. Bill was on the line. He wanted to know where I was.

"Sleeping," I told him.

"You're supposed to be at practice," he said.

I tried to be as straight as I could.

"I don't want to waste my time with a bunch of losers," I said.

He was really upset. Can't say I blame him. Here he was, a first-year head coach, in the toughest media town in the country, with a team that was coming apart on him, and one of his top players giving it to him right between the eyes. The thing was, his ass was as much on the line as any player's. And I think that's why I agreed to go on down to the stadium and meet him. I certainly didn't give a shit about what the Giants might do to me any more than I did about what some of my teammates might think. My attitude was that I played the game a certain way. I didn't need anyone to tell me about playing for my team—I've never been and never will be a selfish player—but losing takes the life out of me. Maybe I'd be a better Raider than a Giant. If the Giants wanted to trade me there, let them do it. I'd tell that to Bill, to George Young, and to the Maras. You can take losing and shove it.

That's what I told Bill when we sat together that day in a car in the parking lot outside Giants Stadium. He was upset, but he knew where I was coming from. He asked me, as a favor, to go back in because he needed me to play and because he wanted to win—badly. I believed that.

Over the years, Bill and I have had an up-and-down relationship. In a lot of ways, we're similar. We're both very emotional and very superstitious. Bill has these routines he goes through—like planting lucky pennies and keeping a bunch of elephant statues in his office with the trunks all pointing to the door—and I have mine. I get my left ankle taped before my right on game day; I always make sure I show only an inch of uniform blue—no more—below the knees. On our final Saturday practice before a game, I have to end things by standing at the fifty-yard line and throwing to someone in the end zone against coverage. I must do that. It's become known on the Giants as "the Saturday bomb." No Saturday bomb, no chance to win on Sunday. Bill has no problem understanding that. I think if I somehow forgot my Saturday bomb, he's just superstitious enough to find me and remind me to go through with it.

Bill calls me "Rose"—has something to do with my college colors—light blue and white being "bathroom colors." Rose, in his mind, is also a bathroom color. So, to him, I'm Rose. We call him Tuna and a few other names, but the way I get back at him is that I bet with him all the time, on anything and everything—golf holes, cards, the exact time of day—because I know he's as much a sucker for competition as I am. He'll tell you he wins nine out of ten, but don't you believe him. He's mine. Nine out of ten times.

I went back to practice after that, but I surely didn't change my ways one bit. I didn't warm up to practice, I hit the bars just as hard, and I hit the field even harder. I didn't give a damn what people said as long as they took note of how I played. On Sundays, I was there for one purpose—and sometimes I made a point of letting my teammates know it, too. From about the end of my second year on, I started going after some players who made mistakes during games. I'd go after them during games, right out in the open. I'd stand there and scream at them, I'd run after them and ream their ass on the sideline, I'd let them know what they cost their team.

Sometimes they would come back at me a little, but most of the time they didn't. I never went after the older players, players who had more seniority—that's a rule I'll always keep for myself—but the younger ones would hear it, just the way I did from Brian during my first year. There was a "closed" team meeting one day in December '83. Things were pretty tight and tense anyway—a number of us in the linebacker corps were by then talking about wanting to leave the Giants—and during this meeting I just tattooed some of the younger players who I thought were regularly messing up.

I never would criticize anyone for making a mistake full tilt, but for mistakes that are made out of laziness or because you think you have things made and don't need to go all out, I'll get on their ass anytime I can. I've been that way forever, and I will be till the day I quit football. It's another system-breaker, I guess: The rules and regulations regarding conduct and behavior have some pious little number about not criticizing teammates, and every coach and his cousin are into the brotherhood of the team. So what? Once in Carolina, during a real close game against Clemson, Steve Streater made some dumb mistake in the defensive backfield that cost us a field goal just before the first half ended. I went after him so hard you wouldn't have believed it. I mean, I knew the man. I knew his store hours better than anyone. I walked up and down the field so everyone from the thirty to the thirty could hear me yelling, "You stupid, beer-guzzling, dumb-ass sonuvabitch, if you'd pay more attention to your goddamned coverage than to the shit you're on, we might win a ball game or two!" I hollered at him all the way into the locker room at halftime and then some more inside as well and on the way out.

I wasn't any kinder to the younger guys on the Giants then, and I know it ticked some of the guys off. Tough shit. Harry apparently got upset about it, said somewhere that I put myself ahead of my teammates, though I don't recall his ever confronting me with that.

Jimmy Burt did confront me, once, twice, any number

of times—about teeing off on guys and about lots of other things, too. Jimmy and I are both cut out of the same cloth; both of us are types who will automatically go for the jugular. I think that may account for why Jimmy and I, over the years, have had something of a strange but intense relationship.

We sometimes argued right out on the field. If Jimmy got ticked off at me, he wouldn't hide it for a minute. We went at it in one game at Giants Stadium sometime in '83 to the point where I *know* the other guys, on both teams, just came to a dead stop and watched with amazement.

The thing about Jimmy—as you might have been able to tell when he went up in the stands after we won the NFC championship—is that winning is his aphrodisiac. He can't do without it any more than I can, and he's one of the toughest sonsuvbitches you'll ever see going after it. I mean, this is a guy who'll get you by the throat and not let up till he's got you. Like me, he will do *anything* to win—and like me, no matter how he ever reacted to my reaming another teammate out, he's a renegade.

A few years ago, Jimmy and I used to play golf together all the time. Naturally we bet and, in those days, before my game really improved, I would lose my shirt to him. He didn't give a shit. He wanted to play $25 to $50 Nassau (match betting with extra for individual holes), and he wouldn't think of lowering the bets. After a while, my game improved to the point where I could take him pretty regularly. Then he wanted to play $5 Nassau. No way I was going to give that to him.

One day we were playing in a tournament together. We were out on the front nine at about the seventh hole, and we had both hit our drives off the tee about three hundred yards down the center of the fairway. Only we had gone to the middle of the wrong fairway. When we realized what had happened, I rode out to pick up our balls. I picked up

Jimmy's, noticed it was a Pinnacle Alpine, and brought it back to him.

We tied the next hole, then teed off on the par-five eighth hole. The match at that point was really close, and for both of us it was grudge all the way. On this particular hole, I hit my drive off to the right, and he duck-hooked one off to the left into some trees. I never saw him go to his ball, but when I came out of the rough we headed in the same direction up near the hole. I couldn't find my ball, so I began looking for it on the other side of a road. Then I noticed a ball lying in the middle of the roadway. It was a Pinnacle Alpine. I picked it up and walked back to Jimmy, who was about to play his next shot.

"Find your ball?" I said.

"Yeah," he said, "here it is." It was a Titleist.

I looked at him.

"Really," I said, "I have one of yours in my pocket." I tossed him his ball. He went red with anger and started swearing up and down that I was accusing him of cheating and that he hadn't been. Now, this was during a tournament, and all of a sudden we got nose to nose, ready to fight—and we would have. But I backed off and told Jimmy he could keep his money. We haven't played golf or been all that friendly since. Jimmy will swear, if you bring it up to him, that I was the one who cheated at golf. But the fact is we just don't hit the links together anymore.

I don't know to this day whether Jimmy is one of the "anonymous" voices on the team who seem willing to let the media know things—like my going after guys in "closed" meetings—that, taken out of context, make me look bad. I couldn't care less about any of that.

I care what kind of a ballplayer Jimmy Burt is, and I tell you this: I respect the hell out of him.

Here's another of my superstitions. When we leave the tunnel to come out on the field, I always have to be the last one out. Not only that, the guy who has to be next to last is Jimmy. If he's not there, I'll find him and pull him back there with me. I won't go out unless he's right in front of me.

In my system, I need Jimmy Burt to win. The only system either of us respects is winning.

15

FOOTBALL is really two games. One takes place on the field, the other takes place in office suites. In both games, there are people playing for keeps—and you had better pay as much attention to the guys in the three-piece suits as to the ones in pads. Both of them want to do to you what you want to do to them. The business side of the game can be as wild as a month of Sundays.

If you're a player, you soon learn that your ass carries a price tag from the day you enter the league till the day you leave. You can choose to ignore it at your own peril. That little tag will wind up hanging from a toe and will read "DOA." On the other hand, you can make sure you get back from the game what you put into it. From day one I was determined to make sure I would never wind up down and out when my career was over. A lot of players have had that happen to them, mistaking the euphoria of playing for cold cash. Watch out for that one.

If Jim McMahon's shoulder doesn't heal, there goes his paycheck and his motorcycle ads. If the Refrigerator doesn't cut down on his between-meal snacks, he may wind up worrying about where his next meal is coming from.

When I originally signed with the Giants, I signed for more money than I had ever seen in my life. My contract was lucrative—as far as the Giants went—but not in terms of the league or, certainly, other professional sports. I had a four-year contract beginning at about $125,000 a year and going up to about $300,000 in my last year. By NFL standards, it was modest given what contribution I made to the team. In those days, I was expected to turn the team around. There wasn't that much help out there, and the load inevitably fell on my shoulders. That was good for neither the team nor myself, but, in any case, that's the way it was and, in the process, I think I gave something to the position I covered that churned things up around the league. I felt the Giants might have fairly recognized that.

Before the '83 season began, I asked the Giants to re-negotiate my contract. I didn't ask them to tear up my old contract, just to extend the one I had for another two years. What I wanted was to have more guaranteed time on the higher end of their payout to me. Injury can wipe out a career on any given Sunday. The average pro football life is a little over four years, the time it takes most kids to learn to stop sucking their thumbs. Football players better get it while they can because glory and awards won't ever cover your ills after you leave the game.

The Giants, true to their traditions, didn't agree with this line of thinking. My agents and I talked the matter over and we decided that I should hold out. I did, for almost three weeks. And I was miserable the whole time. I know it wasn't easy for my teammates either, because they knew as professionals what I was going through and that it had nothing to do with my commitment to playing the hardest game I could—with them. I know they resented statements coming out of management that no one player is more important than the team—which happens to be true but had nothing to do with paying a player what he's worth. One time, maybe a week or so after my holdout began, I took a friend, Bobby Cupo, along with me to camp. I don't really know why I went. I know I was restless, I wanted to be there, and I wanted not to be there. It was like I couldn't keep still.

We went out to Pleasantville and sat high up on a grassy hillside overlooking the practice field. My intention was to be far enough away so that my presence wouldn't create a fuss—either with the fans or with the team. But the guys spotted me up there and the cover was blown. They started pointing to me, waving—and later on, after everyone knew, Harry and some of the other players came out on the field all wearing uniform jerseys with my number 56. I was pleased, but I got out of there. Stirring up a fuss wasn't going to settle things one way or the other.

Another time, I decided to take in one of our preseason games at Giants Stadium. It was against the Jets, and the place was sold out. From the moment I came out of the runway into the stands, I knew my being there was a mistake. People started chanting, "LT! LT!" And then there were other fans, ones who obviously saw me as the epitome of the selfish ballplayer in my fight with management. There was one guy in particular who kept screaming obscenities at me. Linda was with me, could hear every word, and I hated that. But there was no way I was going to respond, even by looking at the guy who was showering down this abuse. I had to physically restrain Bobby, who was with us, because he wanted to go up after the guy. It was all crazy and unreal—the cheering, the abuse, the game on the field. It was the first and only pro game I ever attended in the grandstand, and I wanted to get away as badly as I had wanted to come. I left at halftime.

I don't know if the Giants knew what I might be feeling or not, but they made no move to do much of anything. The more time went by, the more I couldn't stand it. I never felt threatened by what the Giants did or didn't do; I just missed being away from football, and I was making everyone around me pay for my own unhappiness. I told my agents after weeks of it that I wanted to go back—make what arrangements they could, just let me go back and play.

According to the agreement we worked out, the Giants

committed themselves to revising my contract after the season ended. I'm sure that in due course they would have gotten around to it, too. But one day, in the tenth or eleventh week of the season, something else came up. I never saw it coming—and, for sure, neither did the Giants.

I got a call early one morning while I was at home staring at the TV screen. The guy on the other end identified himself as Brig Owens from the NFL Players Association. He said that there was a guy named Jim Gould who was associated with Donald Trump, the real estate developer and owner of the New Jersey Generals, who wanted to talk to me. Would it be okay if he called? I told the guy it would be fine, then hung up and forgot about it. A short while later, the phone rang again and it was this dude named Gould.

"Donald Trump is interested in talking to you," he said, wanting to know if I could come into the city that day at about twelve-thirty for a meeting. As I still saw no problem in any of this, I said fine, I would be there.

Of course, I knew who Donald Trump was, but I really didn't think that what might be involved was an offer to play for the Generals. I still had years to go on my Giants contract with the promise to renegotiate at the end of the season.

I arrived at Trump Tower wearing a suit, I think, but feeling very much like someone from Lightfoot when I saw what was around me. I mean, big-city buildings didn't surprise me that much anymore, but this place was sophisticated New York in capital letters. There was this incredible indoor waterfall, and people were strolling around with violins to a tinkling piano somewhere.

When I got to Trump's office, he wasn't there. Jim Gould was. He kept telling me, while we waited, how great a ballplayer Trump thought I was. It was no secret to me that this meeting was going to involve football, but there was still nothing to do but wait. After a while, the telephone rang. It was Donald. He was calling from his car phone, saying he was caught somewhere in traffic.

I was taken downstairs for lunch. It was all very low-keyed and friendly—and impressive. When Donald finally came, we went back upstairs to his office. He got right to the point. He wanted me to play for him after my contract with the Giants was finished. He told me he was building a dynasty that one day would beat any team in the NFL so that when the two leagues finally merged, a certainty, he said, he hoped I would be playing for him. The defense, he promised, would be built around me. This team would be like no other.

It all sounded just perfect—and so I listened, without intending to get into anything with Trump at all. I told him that I appreciated his interest in me but I would need a little time to think.

No problem there.

A short while later, I accompanied Jim Gould to another office where they had a film all lined up waiting to be shown. It was about Donald Trump the man, and what he had done. It was about Trump Tower and the New Jersey Generals, and it was impressive. Everything that was going on was impressive. Donald Trump was impressive: He was young, dynamic, rich, and very articulate; his offices were impressive, his building was impressive, his film was impressive, this show he was putting on for me was impressive. Then right in the middle of all this, there was another telephone call.

This one just happened to be from Chris Collinsworth, the Bengals' wide receiver who had created a lot of noise when he signed a "future" contract with the USFL. He just wanted me to know, he said—I didn't ask him how he happened to know I'd be in Trump's office—how good a move he had made, how all his financial worries were now over, etc.

Some time later, I was put in touch with a lawyer from Washington, D.C., who had worked out Collinsworth's contract with Trump and who said he could be up in New York the following evening for dinner. I agreed to meet him, still not thinking much about what exactly was going to be offered. At that point I was feeling flattered that Trump thought I was important enough to put on such a show for, but that was it. I was having fun, and I was curious.

But when I met this lawyer the next night at a steak house in the city, the fun and games stopped. We talked cold cash, about what a "future" contract with Trump might look like. When he ultimately got back to me with Trump's exact offer, it all sounded like *Dallas* or *Dynasty*—not the New Jersey Generals. To begin with, the guy talked about bonds and other fancy financial instruments and investments which could legally turn a $1 million loan into $1 million free and clear.

I am legally bound not to disclose the terms of any of the stuff that happened between myself, Trump, and the Giants, so let's just say that as *The New York Times, The Washington Post* and a lot of other papers reported at the time, this represented a $1 million interest-free loan to be paid back in twenty-five years. On top of that, Trump—as reported by the press (let's say conservatively)—offered a four-year deal at $600,000 the first year, then $650,000, $700,000, and $750,000—after my contract with the Giants expired. The $1 million up front, no matter if I got injured in the meantime or wound up having to retire, was mine to keep playing with.

Never mind what the Giants had been doing with me. *That* was an offer. "Give me a day to think about it," I said. It was more like recovery time than thinking time.

"Fine," he said. "No problem."

I couldn't get this offer out of my mind. I didn't believe it was real. You don't just give away money like that. I thought about what I had lost during the strike, what had been going on with the Giants, what was likely to happen—and against all that was this $1 million just for the asking. That meant financial peace of mind for me and my family for a good long time to come, no matter what. I called the guy the next day, without consulting any agents, and said I would go with it.

"No problem," he said. He wasn't exactly talkative, but then again he wasn't dealing in words.

The following morning I got a telegram at home. It was from my bank and it said that $1 million had been deposited in my account. To be precise: $1,000,046.11.

That's what happens among tycoons, I guess. But I didn't feel like a tycoon. I felt like a bank robber.

I eventually got around to calling my agents to tell them that Trump was interested in signing me to a future contract, but I couldn't quite bring myself to say anything about the money or the fact that I had already signed. Ivery, who was then working with Mike Trope, got on the first plane to New York. He knew me and the business well enough to smell smoke—and a lot of it.

I would have told Ivery right out but for the fact that I was still in something of a turmoil over this. I couldn't begin to sort out my feelings about one day having to leave the Giants and the NFL and play in a league I neither knew nor believed in. The Giants to me were far more than management—they also were the guys I played with, the fans I played for, they were my football life. The only real focus I had was that million bucks.

Ivery and I shot the shit, we went here and there, but I somehow couldn't break the ice with him. The way it happened was kind of funny. He had made some passing remark about my car, that I had driven it into the dirt since he had last seen me or something. My response was to suggest that we go look at some new cars. I had wanted to get a BMW for a while anyway, so we went over to this dealer and started looking around. I found the car I wanted, turned to Ivery, and said, "This is nice, right?"

He agreed.

I told him to wait right there and I went to call my bank,

to make sure the million was still there. They assured me it still was. I came back and wrote out a check for the car on the spot and handed it to the dealer. Ivery suddenly seemed to freeze in his tracks.

"Sonuvabitch, you did it," he said.

He didn't mean the car.

I just looked at him and smiled.

What Ivery wanted to know before anything was whether or not I really wanted to play for the Generals. I told him the truth, that I hadn't really considered it. I said that the NFL had been around for all these years and the top salary in the league was somewhere between $300,000 and $500,000 and here was this new league paying twice and three times that just for a "future" contract.

Ivery's position was that if I didn't really want to play for the Generals, we should try to have the Giants buy Trump's contract out. That was fine with me, I said, just so long as that million bucks stayed right in my bank account.

I don't know how much bargaining room I was giving him, but it would have to be enough because there was no way I was going to give that money back. I wasn't a legal expert, but I sure knew that what was in my bank account was reality.

Ivery said that when he told George Young what had happened he thought the man was going to have a heart attack.

"The Giants have never come close to paying out that kind of money," he said.

Ivery told him that if they wanted to buy back the contract—something they said they were interested in—they would realistically have to match Trump's offer. Young said that was a decision he could not make alone, that he would have to be back to us.

Meanwhile, before the press had any real idea of what was going on, I told my teammates. They seemed happy for me. They wished me luck and offered encouragement. Losing any player who helps the team is obviously not something players feel good about—if the team is weakened, their own livelihoods are involved—but there is this larger fraternity of interest in anyone's contract battles with management. That was especially true when what was involved was this new wild card in the football business, the USFL. For the first time since the merger with the old AFL, the NFL was being forced to deal with a competitive salary structure.

By the time the season ended, the story, of course, had broken, though its conclusion was still uncertain because the Giants hadn't yet moved. Instead, I moved—away from everything. Linda and I and a couple of friends hopped a plane and flew down to the Bahamas for a few weeks. As far as I was concerned, I didn't want to hear a word about anything till it was over and done with. I didn't even think about it. I just partied—and partied and partied. When we came back, Trump had been bought out and I had a new contract with the Giants covering not four but six years at even better numbers than Trump had offered.

When I think about it now, it still seems crazy. In one way, this was a story to end all stories about beating the system. I mean, there I was, minding my own business, while people fell all over themselves trying to put mountains of money in my bank account. I didn't solicit their business, I just made damn sure I didn't turn them down. Obviously, without that future offer, I never would have asked for that kind of money from the Giants—and they never would have paid it—but there was Donald Trump and the USFL. Every professional football player in the United States and Canada lost out when the USFL went under because that league was the first real wedge the players had against the tight-money monopoly the NFL has always enjoyed.

I think Donald Trump was brilliant in all this. I mean, I did nothing more than to count my money. This guy dropped a million bucks to me and then in the buyout wound up clearing an *enormous* profit for himself. I mean, he couldn't have made that kind of quick return on the stock market if he had been tight with Ivan Boesky. I don't know if Trump planned it that way from the start, knowing the Giants would never let me go, but I tell you what: Donald Trump has got to be one of the smartest men who ever put on a business suit. It's just too bad he wasn't smart enough to keep the USFL going.

I never would have played for the Generals. If the Giants lost anything in this deal, they, not me, will have to say. I tell you, when I look at a full stadium every week and at the figures for the league's television revenue, I don't worry too much about them. Without that, I would have quit after my contract with them ran out—which my agreement with Trump would have permitted. At that point, all my football friends were on the Giants. Winning or losing, they had become a kind of family, like Carolina, and even though the NFL can never be like college, if you are around people you care for long enough, you don't want to leave them. You earn a livelihood together, you share good times and bad, you are competing together against the best, intimate with winning and losing in ways that others outside the family will never quite know or understand.

The Giants were my place of professional pride. Everything I had earned as a professional came from them. Everything I stood to lose was bound up with them, too. I was glad to have my future guaranteed with them.

The future I almost lost with drugs.

16

THE first time I used drugs in the pros, it was cocaine, and I didn't pay attention to it any more than I did when I had my first beer. I'm not even sure now when that first moment was because it really seemed so insignificant at the time. What I do remember was going to a party sometime in October 1982. It was a Halloween party and instead of jellybeans and pumpkin pie there were drugs everywhere. You would not believe the variety and the volume of the stuff that was around or the people who were into it.

Of course I wasn't surprised that professional ballplayers used drugs. I don't happen to believe that drugs are a unique problem in football or any other professional sport. There are drugs in the media, drugs in police departments, and drugs in the Senate. Look around you, you can have some.

The Giants, like every other team in the NFL, had guys who did drugs and guys who didn't. I knew some of them, I didn't know others. Pretty nearly everybody knew about me because I made no effort to hide it.

Looking back on it, there's a part of me that's still unbelieving. I didn't like drugs in college. I stayed away from them even though they were available. I occasionally smoked marijuana but really didn't like it because it would make you unable to comprehend what was going on around you. To this day, I can't stand the smell of weed. It makes me sick. My best friends in college, who were into herb, used to kid me about it all the time.

When I got to the Giants, there was a friend on the team who always had cocaine around and who kept trying to get me to use it. For a long time, I had no interest.

When I started, it was just part of a good time. I got high on the stuff, but hell, I drove my car over a hundred miles an hour, closed down more bars than I can remember, went where I wanted, and did what I wanted and still could go out on a football field and knock some dick loose. Cocaine was illegal, that was true. I wasn't *supposed* to be doing it, there was this and that campaign against it, every politician, police chief, and Nancy Reagan were against it—but hell, with a guy like me, that almost made it more attractive. Tell me no and I'll argue and fight you—just to be different. It doesn't matter over what. I was born in Virginia, but I'm from Missouri. You've got to show me.

For a long time, well into the '84 season, I had no sense at all that I *needed* cocaine to get by. I didn't. I could do it and I could stop it. I also knew that I was going to quit at some point, but I couldn't say when. It's even possible I had to get into trouble first because everything I've ever done that's mattered to me, I've done under pressure. But when I look back on this period of recreational use of cocaine, there was no pressure to do anything other than to go with it.

I never thought or intended to get to a point where I would be addicted. In my entire life, I never let anyone or anything control me. An occasional line of coke sure wasn't about to do it. I knew what I was doing, knew how to take the stuff and how much to use. In those early years I regularly used about a half a gram every two to four weeks and made damn sure to stay away from nasty sutff like free-basing and needles. Later on I wound up using an eighth or more in a single evening. And the shit was a lot heavier.

Now, the thing in common about the Giants, the NFL,

the FBI, the CIA, and your local neighborhood cops is that they all have a pretty good idea of what's going on. But then what do they do about it? From very early on, the Giants knew who on the team was into drugs. They certainly knew I was because they let me know. I have a friend whose brother is a lawyer who works closely with law enforcement. Through my friend, I had word passed—from the police—that *they* knew what I was doing. I used to get followed—to bars, to parties, to and from practices and games. Cops and NFL security people, people I knew, would follow me. This wasn't paranoia on my part, this was surveillance—and it was a joke. I had another friend, a reporter out of L.A., who knew that all those people knew. I had never told him a thing.

You can probably guess by now what my attitude toward all this was. If they wanted to bust me, fine. But I knew they weren't going to do that, not as long as I was who I was and my game was intact. If I were Joe Blow, okay, there'd be the slammer or some midnight trip to Betty Ford's farm. But I felt, as far as playing ability went, I could do pretty nearly anything I wanted to on a football field and that that carried over to the rest of my life. It was almost a thrill in itself knowing that people knew what I was doing and wouldn't do a damn thing to stop me.

What did happen was that a lot of other guys on the team began to cool out. The Giants had started to move against them. Perk, when he was coach, and now Bill had let it be known that drugs would not be tolerated on the team. After Bill got through his first year—and wasn't fired—he started cleaning house. He got rid of everyone he thought was on drugs except me, along with some other guys whose only crime might have been their closeness with me. By the end of the '84 season, I looked around one day and found that every friend I had on the team was gone—traded, released, or cut. What was I supposed to make of that? I certainly felt hurt and depressed to lose my friends. But I wasn't about to change my ways. Besides, I knew no one out there was going to stop me.

But then I started to have little subtle changes in my thinking about drugs. I started giving myself excuses to use cocaine. It maintained my weight, it did this, it did that. I knew that physically I was all right—my body told me so. I could go out there the way I always had. Drugs didn't have anything to do with my game, only I kept finding these excuses to use the stuff. When I took cocaine, things got quiet for me. I had never felt that kind of quiet and peace before. When I would come down from it, I got unhappy that it had to be over. I don't know when exactly, but there was a time when I began to realize that it just wasn't true when I told myself that I didn't have to do it again. That was the subtlest change of all. I told Linda—no one else—that I thought I might be getting myself hooked. I didn't know what to do about it.

In minicamp before the '85 season, my urine turned up dirty. That gave the Giants more maneuvering room than they had had in the past with me. Until then, they had been powerless to act because they had no proof of anything— only hearsay. In the NFL at that point, one urine test a year was permitted under the collective bargaining agreement. But if a player tested positive, the club was allowed thereafter to test randomly. The Giants had what they needed to try to rein me in. That, by the way, is how the club and the league can both keep things quiet and still come after you. There are plenty of dirty-urine tests every year that no one finds out about but that keep the player who is caught on the high wire between the club and the league.

Bill's response was to try to help me. I don't know what, if anything, he did with respect to the league, but he got someone in New York to help me. I went for a short while, but that didn't work. I didn't want the Giants or the NFL to have anything to do with this—I knew from the start what that meant. I didn't want them in on anything, I didn't want them paying for anything, it was *my* problem, and I was going to handle it my way—if I could.

The problem was, I didn't quite yet see it as a real problem—other than having to pass urine tests whenever and wherever the Giants or the league decided to give them. I needed to do that to get people off my back. That was the system. And I had to beat it.

The way I beat urine testing was simple: I never used my own. I kept a little aspirin bottle handy, and when they announced a drug test, I'd get a teammate who I knew was clean to piss for me. I'd then put the aspirin bottle into my jock, get my test bottle, go off to a stall, and give them back clean piss. There was one time they even announced they were going to do a test under observation—that is, with some dude standing right at my back while I faced the urinal. I beat that, too, with a soft squeeze bottle, a Visine container. When I stood at the urinal, it was just a matter of reaching down and squeezing the bottle instead of my dick. Sherlock Homes would have needed a second time to figure that one out. (Strangely enough, the really tough urine tests came last summer, when I had been through rehab and was absolutely clean. By then, everybody in the country knew I had had "a problem," and it felt like everybody in the country was standing around the urinal when I went in there to piss. I mean, there would be guys flunking their tests and *everyone* was waiting to see me tap out my full bottle.)

The thing about cocaine is that it doesn't affect you quite the same way over a long period of time. The more you use it, the more these subtle changes continue. I started to need that quietness, I could feel mellow and unhurried—and then there was this thing with time. It was like I would tell myself I would just stop off for a while, intending to stay no more than an hour and then go home. One hour, I found, would become four—or eight—and I wouldn't realize it. I would be somewhere half the night and then turn up at dawn to face Linda and the kids, thinking that I had intended to go out for only an hour.

I began to get paranoid rather than just mellow. Where was I? Who were the people I was with? I didn't know them all—my friends had started to change, I was no longer hanging out with other football players. I would go places with people I barely knew. Could they be cops? Was the place we went to going to be raided? What were those sounds in the next apartment? There were people more strung out than I was, guys who were so paranoid they would sit facing the front door with guns dangling in their hands, waiting for the cops or rival dealers.

I started to do more and more stuff during the '85 season. Where I had been using a half a gram over a month, I was using a good part of that in a single evening. I began to stay out for longer and longer periods of time. I came home at four, five, six o'clock in the morning—and then I wouldn't come home at all. It would get so late that I'd just stay where I was, sleep it off, get up, do some more, and watch the day turn into night before I realized that a day—or even two—had gone.

Linda—and my friend Paul, who had been cut from his last pro team and was living with us—got crazier and crazier because of this. They used to drive around trying to find me when I didn't come home. They drove to all the spots they knew I might have gone, and they wouldn't find me. They sometimes spent an entire night out on the streets, looking. If you don't want to be found, you won't be.

Sometimes I did. I called Paul once and told him to get me because my truck had broken down. When he got there, God knows what time, I told him before he could open his mouth, "Don't even say a word, I know I did bad. Just get me home—and for goodness sake, keep Linda away from me."

Poor Mr. Davis. He didn't know what to make of me, and his position in the house was difficult for him, I know.

He got out books on drug abuse, read them, tried to learn from them so he could help me. But there wasn't much he could do.

Linda would fuss, and she would forgive me. Linda forgave me more times than she had any right to, more times than I could bear. I couldn't stand what I was putting her through. I know from the way she looked—she didn't need words—that she was going through a hell that was probably as bad as the one I was going through. I could see her getting more and more tired. Her face looked drawn and her eyes were sometimes red and swollen because she had been crying.

But she kept forgiving me. I'd come home after two, maybe three days away, and I'd swear I'd never do it again. And then two days later, I'd be out again, meaning to be home after just a little while, and days would pass, somewhere, somehow, in places I hardly knew. And when I was home, I shouldn't have been. My son and daughter looked at me like they didn't know me. I can't ever forget that. Oh, I was still Daddy to them, but it was like I had become a stranger. I could see fear in their eyes. It killed me—and I couldn't do anything to stop it. Except move out of my house.

For two weeks, I moved in with my friend Bobby Cupo. Bobby tried to stay with me every minute I wasn't on a football field in an effort to keep me away from drugs. He drove me to practice and he picked me up. We went bowling, barreling around, but he could no more stop me than I could myself.

The hell of it was that through much of this, I felt I still could play good ball. My '85 season was another Pro Bowl season—I led the team in just about every defensive category, had over a hundred tackles, and had more sacks—13½—than I had gotten in a single season before. Later on, the media started dissecting my season, trying to show how substance abuse might have been involved. I mean, they were vicious—and they were off. They remembered that I used to weave my car in and out among the parking barrels in the lots outside our practice field. They were right, except that I had been doing that ever since my first year. They wrote that I went to sleep in meetings. Right again, except that I had been doing that, along with a lot of other guys, since my first year. They wrote all kinds of stuff with just enough half truth in it to make it look like the whole truth. I will never apologize for the season I had, something I believe the media are still waiting for me to do.

My body *did* begin to tell me that I could not continue as I was. I knew that I was no longer going at 100 percent. But I also knew that my 75 percent was better than most other guys' 100 percent. When you put out from week to week, when you go at people the way I do and have them go at you as hard as they can, you pay all the dues you need to pay to anyone. I gave my body to the game as much as I ever had.

But I was caught now. Twice a month became three times a week and maybe more. Some of my new friends came right out of the woodwork, glad to get high with "LT"—it beat getting my autograph any day. I went to places that were down and out with people who were down and out, and I didn't give a shit. I was paranoid and strung out and my body was screaming out at me to stop—and I couldn't.

I began to use heavy stuff—crack—because the high was much more intense. I did crack from the middle of the '85 season to the end, usually when we were at home. I'd stay out all night, get blasted on crack and then try to pick up as though nothing had happened the next day. I did crack too many times to count and more times than I want to remember—and it finally left me with the feeling that I had had the shit kicked out of me before I ever set foot on a football field.

I don't know how long I could have gone on that way. I am certain that if it had been much longer, I would have lost my family and my career and maybe my life. I do know that I had reached a point where an accumulation of subtle changes had added up to the biggest one of all. I had been a man who had never been controlled by anyone or anything, and now I was being controlled by a little ball of junk that I could roll around between my thumb and forefinger.

Linda literally saved me. The one thing about Miss Cooley is that she is every bit as tough in her own way as I am. She was at the point where she was not only tired but also tired of forgiving me—which was long past the point where any wife or any lover would have stayed with you— and she got in her car one night when I didn't come home. This time, instead of driving aimlessly around, she had called up different friends and found one who thought he knew where I might be. She had had him drive out to this place, and he had come back and said that he saw my truck there.

I was in an apartment, in a back room, totally out of it. There were some other people there, doing what I don't know. Then Linda got there. I heard her voice in the outer room, and someone was telling her I wasn't there. She was saying she knew I was there, and then she found my hat. I could feel her coming toward the door, and I started to close it. She pushed against it.

"I'll break the damn door down if you don't open it, Lawrence Taylor!"

"Get the fuck out of here!" I shouted. I tried to force the door closed. But her body was between it and the wall.

"I'm not leaving till I leave with you!" she screamed. "You're going home with me!"

Linda then proceeded to kick the damn door open. She literally kicked her way into the room. Oh, Miss Cooley!

"You're coming with me," she said. "You're going home."

I went with her. That was the first step I took toward saving myself.

17

AFTER I went into rehabilitation in March 1986, the Giants released a statement in my name. I talked about a difficult and ongoing battle to overcome my problems, along with my determination to dedicate myself anew to football. It was a good statement, written by Bill Parcells, I think. At the time, I was in no condition to agree or disagree with anything in it.

I had told Linda and Paul for a long time that I wanted to get help. But I couldn't move on it till Linda finally threatened me with the one thing she knew would get me off my ass. She said she would tell my mother. And she did after that night she brought me home. Outside my own family, my mother is the closest person to me in the world. I couldn't bear the idea of her finding out. She had put so much into her own children, she had been there so many times—like a guardian angel—when things could have blown up on me, she had been a friend and a supporter, she had endured years of hard times and my father's anger in order to hold her family together, that I simply could not face the idea of shaming her in this way.

But I knew that I had to face it—and not just because my mother had found out. When Linda confronted me four days after the Pro Bowl that year (I also had been reminded in Hawaii by other players how widely known my problem had become), I called Ivery down in Houston and told him what had happened and that I wanted to find some kind of clinic where I could go. The most important thing, I said, was for me to be out of New York. There were so many friends of mine who were into drugs, it was so available, I needed to go away, to sit down where my time would be monitored and there would be people around watching me. If I was allowed to run free, I would run wild. At that point I wasn't thinking about fans or football or anything—I was thinking about saving myself if I could. The people I thought about had nothing to do with football—Linda and Paul and my parents and D'Fellas and my teachers and friends in Williamsburg.

Ivery said he would try to find something for me, and meantime I took a trip down to the Burg. When Ivery called back to say he had found a place for treatment, I delayed going. I spent two weeks in Williamsburg before I went to Houston. For most of the time I was home, my folks never brought up anything, even though my mother was dying to. My pop had said to her that the most important thing they could do for me was to make sure I knew that I could go home, that home was a place of refuge where no explanations were necessary. But I knew how much my mother wanted to ask me about what was going on, because she talked regularly to one of D'Fellas, Eric Stone—and she let him know. One night, a day or two before I left Williamsburg, I was sitting in the kitchen with my mom and I brought the subject up. She nearly burst.

"Lonnie, I thought you'd never say anything!" she said.

I told her as much as I could. I didn't want to go into details, but I didn't want either of my folks ever getting things secondhand from the media. I didn't want them having to make guesses about where I was going or what I had to do. I know my mom understood a lot of what I was feeling—because she knew me so well—but I knew how worried she was even while she was offering me all the support she could. In the old days she might have sent me for a switch to go along with the understanding, but now she could only sit by and listen. But I could see what was in her eyes. She was praying for me.

I went to Williamsburg because I needed to. This was where I came from. Down here I wasn't LT, football player, but Lawrence or Lonnie or just plain Taylor.

I went to my high school, Lafayette, just as I did every year after the football season. I've donated a bit of my money to upgrade the football program there. I have a scholarship program that yearly provides for full four-year college support to a graduating male and female student. Coach Jones has me talk to his students. People are proud of me down in the Burg, and it hurt me to feel the hurt I might be causing them.

As I always did, I sat in on my old teachers' classes. I didn't need to make a fuss about it. As always, I just sat through lessons to listen—and this time to remember as well.

Mr. Stokes still teaches his government class. Mr. Stokes was such a good teacher, and he put up with so much. He once had been our baseball coach and he lost his job because he just wouldn't keep the lid on for the sake of keeping the lid on. After the last game of one season, we had some beer aboard our team bus. We were having a fine old time that day, so fine that halfway home some of the guys started mooning out the windows as we rolled along. One guy dropped his bare ass right by a parked police car, and that got us pulled over to the side of the road. The cops who caught up to us boarded the bus, smelled the fumes of booze, turned up the cases of beer in the back, and came down heavy on poor Mr. Stokes. Mr. Stokes was a good baseball coach, a good teacher of civics and government, and a good person. He was someone who made me care about school when I could have hated it.

I sat in on my old English class—Mrs. Mayfield had been so damned hard on me while I was in school. I mean, there was no way I had ever been able to get past her. You couldn't fool her, couldn't cheat, couldn't goldbrick—only do the work, do it till she said it was right.

And where was old Mr. West? He was something else again. We were a class of wild people with him. He taught mechanical engineering, and to this day I know things about drawing architectural plans that I probably never would have learned anywhere else. Because our school had no windows, one flip of the lights would plunge a room into darkness. We used to flip the lights on Mr. West and start throwing things around the room just for the hell of it. But so did he. *He* would knock the lights out and start things flying! Mr. West is no longer at Lafayette. A few years ago, he was arrested because it turned out that, on the side, he was the ringleader of a gang of bank robbers—the P. West Gang, they were called. I guess school pay wasn't enough. I can laugh and feel sorry and remember, also, that learning happens in ways you never fully appreciate till later on. Mr. West helped me understand how to put a dream about a house onto a piece of paper.

And being home meant, of course, that I could hang out with my boys. We went out and played basketball, we got plenty of beer, we played cards till all hours of the night, and we hit a club or two. They kept me occupied and away from drugs. They were worried about me, I know, but they were with me 100 percent. The thing about all of us is that if any one of us has trouble, all the others know it instantly. You can't hide from D'Fellas.

They had no sermons for me. They had themselves— which is all I was looking for. I didn't know it at the time, but a month before, the guys had all gotten together and decided that only one of them would speak directly to me about drugs.

For two days, I took a detour to Winston-Salem to be with the one Fella who couldn't be there, John Morning. J.D., I knew, was their elected spokesman—and I knew why.

Three years before, when he was visiting me in New York, I asked him at one point to reach over into a pocket of a coat and get what was there. It was my stash.

"What the hell is this?" J.D. had said. "We don't do that shit. We drink a ton of beer, get drunk, sing, and that's it."

J.D. was such a tough sonuvabitch, too. I didn't know what he'd do now. He's a little guy, maybe 5-8 and 160 pounds. He says I'm big and agile and he's small and agile. He says that because he's no more afraid of me than I am of him. We once tore up a fancy hotel room—in one of the Sheratons—just because we felt like getting in a fight. I think I won because I put my head down and drove into his chest, knocking him flat, but he was quicker than a lot of NFL quarterbacks. And nastier.

J.D. certainly did remind me of who we were and who we weren't. But that came later. When he saw me in my wraparound shades and three days' growth of beard, he said, "Man, I love ya."

Then he reamed me out. But when I left, I had been with him almost three days, and because he had been with me all the time, he said something else: "You didn't touch a drop of shit. You're not addicted to anything, Taylor." I wish I could have been so sure.

When I finally took off for Houston, I didn't know what to expect. I didn't really have my hopes up, and I was having second thoughts every step of the way. I was leaving home, going to a strange place, putting myself in someone else's hands. I knew all about the drug horror stories that were around, the Micheal Ray Richardsons and all the others. There was a common belief that once an athlete entered rehabilitation, his career was over. And I also knew that there were plenty of people in the league and on the Giants, from the top right on down, who were hoping I'd never make it, that I'd fall on my face and wind up being cut or traded. I had stepped on an awful lot of toes in five years.

I got a People Express flight out of Newark late one Friday night. I felt like a person running from the law. I wore sneakers, a dark, ratty old overcoat, and shades—even though it was the middle of the night. The whole idea was not to be recognized, who knows if I succeeded.

Ivery says that I didn't look anonymous, I just looked like hell. The game plan was to put me into the hospital as soon as possible. I told him that I wanted to cool out for just a bit. I was feeling so strange, like I was in a dream. I couldn't bring myself just to get on with it. Finally, on Saturday, Ivery said he had been in touch with the doctor who was going to treat me and that they wanted me to check in the following afternoon, on Sunday.

I was placed in Methodist Hospital, a big medical center that has a drug rehabilitation unit within it. I remember that day so well. We went directly to look at this room that I was going to stay in. We got out of an elevator and we walked out onto a regular hospital floor. There were old people strapped into wheelchairs and there was that smell that runs through hospital corridors everywhere. My room was small and dingy. There was a bed and a chair, no other furnishings. No TV, no telephone.

And there were bars on the windows.

I was so sick and angry, I wanted to kick Ivery's ass on the spot.

"I'm not staying here! No way!" I told him. I felt betrayed. Ivery and the doctor looked panicked. They asked me to just take it easy and please to wait. They left me there alone in the room and went off somewhere.

I sat on the edge of this bed, staring out a window that overlooked some woods. My mind was racing, but all I could fix on was having to get out of there immediately. Whatever anybody else decided, I was not going to be caged. If I stayed in a room like this, my drug problem would be twice as bad, I'd wind up ODing or wanting to kill myself—or someone else. I didn't know what was being decided out there, but I was ready just to get up and walk out.

When Ivery came back, I started right in on him. "There's no way in hell I'm staying here! You just get me a plane ticket back to New York and I'm gone!" I said.

The doctor said he understood what I was feeling and asked if I would be willing to look at another part of the hospital where I might be more comfortable. I agreed, but I wasn't expecting much now.

We went to the other side of the building, to an area up on the twelfth floor—it had a name, something like Twelfth-Floor Foundra—strictly for rich folks. I mean, it was a hospital wing, it had heart patients up there and people who were undergoing X-ray treatments, but it was another kind of environment. I think that half the reason people die in hospitals is because of what they see around them; but not in this place.

The room I was shown was huge—it had a big, comfortable bed, sofas, reading chairs, TV, VCR, room service till midnight. It was a hotel suite, not a hospital room. The doctor told me how much more expensive this would be, but money just then wasn't my problem. I told him the room would be fine.

There was one more problem: my identity. I didn't want anyone finding out I was in drug rehab, so I had made sure in advance that the doctor and the hospital would go along with some necessary deception at the time of my admission. The first room I was shown and this one were both apart from the area where drug patients were normally kept. That was okay. My papers would show that I was admitted to the hospital for a stomach disorder requiring extensive testing. I also hoped my name would be kept out of all this.

The hospital agreed to admit me under the name of Paul Davis. For the time I was there, less than a week, everybody called me Paul, including Mr. Davis himself when he came down to visit me.

18

WHAT the hell is rehabilitation, anyway? I wish I had answers, but I don't. I can't say what works and what doesn't work, because I can only speak for myself. If I could get on a moral high horse and say this is what you do, this is what you don't do, fine. But I'm not that kind of person. I don't know what works for you. I know what happened with me, and that's about all I can talk about.

Before anything else happened, I had a whole series of medical tests. I guess this was standard, especially as I was in there supposedly for a stomach disorder. I spent a day giving blood, having X rays taken; at the end I felt more like a lab rat than a person. Actually, these tests turned up some sort of stomach disorder—surprised the hell out of me—but it didn't get me confused about why I was there.

I had pretty much free rein of the place. I could go downstairs and work out in a gym—shoot baskets, lift a few weights—or I could sit around watching TV or reading, even get out for dinner, with a staff person, if I wanted. I met with this psychologist, Dr. Mirabi, each of these first days. That was about it.

We didn't talk about drugs as such, only what might have led me to them in the first place. It was his contention—and I believe it—that what's behind the taking of drugs is just as important as the drugs themselves. In my case, it wasn't too hard to see that drugs were a way of escaping rather than dealing with my problems—the pressures of playing in a huge place like New York, having to please so many people, having to work out a life with my family. I was a person who did anything he wanted at any time he wanted. If I was going to survive, if I was going to hold on to the family I loved, I would have to make adjustments—while still being the person I was. Easier said than done.

After a couple of days the doctor wanted me to go down to a "work group." One of the things that had come up was how hard it was for me to deal with people, no matter who they were, and so he thought working in a group would be good for me to try.

This group was organized like AA—they had all kinds of work sessions where people sat around together talking about their addiction problems. I remember the first day I went down there. I remember the first day because it was also the last day.

I walked into this room and there were all kinds of people—old people, alcoholics, all sitting together looking me over. I was by far the youngest person in the room. The thing is, you're supposed to welcome new members, make them feel at home and warmly supported. They were all into that—like it was religion. One person after another started saying, "How you doing, Mr. Davis?" Every one of them drawled it real slow and loud, like I had a hearing problem or that my brain might have been fried by drugs.

These people were all crazy, I told myself. I couldn't tell what drug and alcohol problems they had, but from their behavior and speech, I knew they were all in serious trouble. There were fifteen or twenty people in this group along with a couple of doctors, and when they started talking about what bothered them, I knew *I* was in trouble. I mean, I was sitting there trying to sort out things about my family, my kids, the media, the fans, New York, the National Football League, my career—and this lady and guy get into an argument because the guy thought he didn't get enough time to say what he wants because the group leader talked too much. Everybody started yelling and screaming about it, taking sides, getting their two cents in—like a bunch of crazies. I mean, I have problems up the ass, and the big thing these folks were worried about was *who talks too much*. I just got up and walked out.

One of the group leaders came right after me. Where was I going? she wanted to know.

"You better take care of the people in there, because they're crazy," I said—and kept on walking.

The doctors asked me to go to another group—for handicrafts. I tried this for a little while, with no better results. I sat around in a room where a bunch of people were working with leather—and the idea was to get you concentrated on things like beltmaking so your mind would be switched from your drug tracks to ones that ran a little straighter. I told Linda and Paul about it and right away they put in their orders for belts from me. Sure thing!

I explained to the staff that I wasn't going to make any belts. I sat around in this room and I just doodled. I drew, I poked at my leather strips—and then finally I got up and started walking around. I'm sure these people thought I was just as crazy as I thought they were.

At the end of this class, the instructor said, "All right, now everyone put your equipment away." It was like he was talking to children. I started to clean my area when I noticed that this woman—her name was Joyce—was having trouble handling a hammer she had been working with. The instructor was standing over her, explaining, "Now, you know where the hammer goes, Joyce. You see the picture of the hammer on the pegboard. You put the hammer right there, where the picture is."

This woman had to be about fifty and she was whining over and over, "I can't, I can't, I just don't know how it goes."

The instructor was full of patience and sweetness. This was religion, remember, not arts and crafts.

"You can do it, Joyce! You can do it!"

"No, I can't. I just can't."

"Yes, you can! Just try!"

Joyce kept moaning, the therapist kept pleading, and I kept wondering how the hell she could *not* be able to put the doggone hammer back on the board. Finally I couldn't take it anymore. I took the hammer away from the woman and slammed it into place on the pegboard.

"That's how it goes!" I yelled. Everybody in the room stopped what they were doing. "That's how the damned hammer goes, right here, like that!" The therapist looked at me like I was going to go off on him or something—I mean, the look he had in his eye was the one Ron Jaworski or Neil Lomax get. I was just trying to preserve my own sanity. I turned and walked out of the room.

I told the doctor that if I stayed there much longer, I might wind up being crazy and not able to play ball anymore. He was sympathetic and didn't try to push me into anything. They gave me freedom to take things a little easy. One afternoon I was let out to shoot a round of golf. I still was meeting with this doctor for an hour or two every day—and that was what counted.

But then one day, a couple of things happened that made even this routine seem like too much. Someone, a hospital worker or staff member, passed me in the hall and said, "Hi, Lawrence." Till then I had more or less believed that my cover was holding. Then, right around the same time—a Thursday or Friday of this same week—Howard Cosell broke the story that I was in drug rehabilitation somewhere.

Now, I have to say that that particular item, apart from the immediate sense of panic it caused, gave me an idea of where things stood. How could someone like Cosell find out that I was in rehab? Because I might be sued for libel, I can't answer my own question. But let's say I know who knew where I was. The number of people who might have been involved was small—my family; my closest friends, including one ex-friend; and a few people on the Giants. I'm sure I know who *didn't* tell Howard Cosell.

I was able to go home for the weekend—to Ivery's house in Houston, that is. I was supposed to return to Methodist again on Sunday evening, but while I was away, I decided that that was it, I wasn't going back. It wasn't just fear of discovery, either. In the week I had spent there, I didn't find any reason to stay, I didn't feel that I had been helped. I called this doctor and told him and we worked something out where I would come in to see him as an outpatient—and that was that. I continued to see Dr. Murabe over the next few weeks, the emphasis always on the substance of my daily life, like my marriage and my career, rather than on the chemical substances I had been using. But from then on, I entered a new and different kind of therapy. It was as improvised as football for me had always been, and like my game, it had plenty to do with impulse and luck.

Let me say right off that without Ivery I don't think I would have gotten through this phase of my recovery. Because I was on the outside and could find my way back to drugs with the touch of a telephone dial, Ivery decided that he was not going to let me leave his sight. He stayed with me literally every minute of every day for the next six weeks—a length of time long enough for me to go clean and for both of us to want to go at each other's throat.

There was never any talk of changing my attitudes about drugs or drinking—not from the doctor and not from Ivery. The doctor kept me focused on those things in my life that led me to drugs. Ivery kept me away from drugs. We played golf. We played a hell of a lot of golf. We'd get up at six o'clock in the morning, play nine holes on one course, get in our car, go to another club for another eighteen or thirty-six holes. We'd watch movies, we'd shop, we'd cook. The sonuvabitch turned out to be a neat freak, and he even made me tidy and pick up after myself.

For about ten days Linda and Paul had come down to visit. That made me feel more at peace, more at home being away from home. But Houston was just a temporary base, anyway. After Cosell's announcement, it was only a matter of time before my whereabouts would be discovered. Once that happened, I would have the damned media horde on my back. My therapy—not recommended for anyone else—was mainly to enjoy myself as much as I could, to live not like a sick or confined person—which the books and the theories tell you you should when you're addicted—but like a healthy person, able to make choices, in relative peace and freedom.

My thing—which goes all the way back to who I am and where I came from—was that no one or no thing controls me. The most basic choice I had to make now was whether or not I would continue to let drugs control me. I chose not to let them. That was first. The next choice was almost as basic. I chose not to kiss anyone's ass.

I stood on the golf course with my beer in my hand and I thought of all those media and management people scurrying around trying to figure out what tank I was in, what detox I was doing, and I enjoyed every minute of it. The golf course was my detox tank.

What Ivery said—and I agreed with it—was that if we wanted to avoid being discovered, we would not be able to stay in one place. The best chance we had of keeping people away was to stay away ourselves. Shortly after I got out of the hospital, leaving most of it to impulse, we started traveling around—like a touring show or guys who had time on their hands, money to burn, and a willingness just to get up and go whenever they felt like it.

See America, cure yourself of drugs!

One day, Ivery said he wanted to go out to Los Angeles to move some furniture he had there back to Houston. He asked another friend, Kenny Burroughs, to join us. We flew out, rented a truck, loaded in his furniture, and took off for Texas. Because there were three of us, the idea was that we would be able to share the driving. Seemed like fun for all. Even though the guys knew me, they felt they'd be in no jeopardy on the road when I drove. You can't take a rental truck over sixty miles an hour. But we had rented cheap, not U-Haul or Avis. "Cheap Heap" meant one less safety feature than the guys, I know, were counting on: a speed governor. The one in this truck was broken. Ivery and Kenny then tried to keep me away from the wheel—they said they would drive the whole way.

But they couldn't do it. Like the guy in the movies who's been guarding his prisoner too long, each one started to nod out. When Ivery went, he climbed in the back, said he was going to sleep and to wake him up when we got to heaven. Kenny had no staying power at all. When he gave up, he slouched down in the front seat and put a hat over his eyes. We went through the desert like an ole cartoon roadrunner. Whee!

Another time, we decided to slip down to Austin for a day or two. Ivery might have had some business there, I don't remember, but there's a really beautiful golf course in Austin. The thing about golf is that when you get out on the course, you really are away from the crowds. The game is very peaceful and very challenging both. You have time to see things and hear things you normally forget about when you're busy. And you have time to concentrate, just concentrate on making your game better. Well, the Austin Country Club that day was nice and deserted—except for one familiar figure who was trailing along in a group behind us. I kept looking and looking and damned if I didn't know that walk and that hat. It was Tom Landry, the coach of the Cowboys. This was too good to be true.

Everybody in the league at that point believed I was drying out in a hole somewhere. So you could say I had this power of surprise going for me. I hung back and waited for the coach to move up a little closer. Then I walked up to him and just as sweet as anything said, "Hi, Coach Landry. How're ya doin'?"

Now, Tom Landry's the kind of guy who will look air conditioned in the middle of a tropical heat wave. But I could see his little eyes light up like he was saying to himself, "What the fuck are you doing here? You're supposed to be in an institution." Instead he said, "Hi, Lawrence, nice to see you. How's everything?"

"Fine, Coach, just fine."

This scene got repeated in one way or another—never as dramatically—right across the country. One time I met a group of people who knew me from New Jersey. I ran into officials, businesspeople, people associated with the league, folks who simply recognized my face and put it together with what they had recently learned from the media. Sometimes the looks I'd get would make me think of a person in a bathtub who had an electrical appliance accidentally dropped next to him in the water.

I felt like a nomad or a gypsy—and I felt free. We lived mainly away from hotels, sometimes in condos—and nearly always out by a golf course. In the mornings we'd get up and decide what we wanted to do that day. If we felt like moving, we'd move—get on an airplane or rent a car and go someplace. If we felt like staying where we were, we'd roll right on out to the golf course.

One time in Florida, we went to a local Baptist church to hear a gospel chorus sing. The mother of this friend of mine was in the chorus, and I remember sitting there with Ivery listening to this music—I happen to love gospel music—and getting into an argument with him over which one of us was crying. This chorus was out of sight and it was no shame for anyone to sit there carrying on, but old Ivery, to this day, swears that he could see tears rolling down my face, while I *know* that tears were coming down his face. I mean, I had my wraparound shades on and I will admit to some foam around the edges of my eyes, but I'll be damned if Ivery could see through my glasses.

Another time we went on up to Alabama. Ivery had some business there and so did I. In Tuscaloosa, I called my old coach Ray Perkins and told him I was in town. I wanted to speak to him; he and Bill Parcells were the only people in football to whom I felt I owed some kind of explanation. I wasn't looking for advice from Perk; I didn't expect him to understand or condone anything I had done. He was an intense football person, a guy who *expected* you to cut off your arm for the game. I had played like that for him, and I had had his respect.

I was supposed to meet him at the golf course we were playing that day, but he was not there when we started our round. I don't exactly know whether it was coming to the ninth or the eighteenth hole, but I was just stepping out of the woods looking for a lost ball when I saw this golf cart put- putting across the fairway from the clubhouse. There was one guy riding in it, and it was Perk.

We went on back to the clubhouse, pulled up a couple of chairs on the front porch, and sat there talking for an hour or so. I told him what had happened so he would be sure he had gotten the story from me and not from the media.

Perk, for his part, was disappointed. I expected nothing less. The man is so straight, and football for him is the epitome of straight living. Whatever he had to say would begin and end with football. Perk felt that I owed an explanation to the fans and that I should speak to the press. He didn't have much more to say. I thanked him for listening to me, we shook hands, and we went our different ways again.

I never felt I could make my way back with an explanation or with words. I respected Ray, but I couldn't follow his suggestion. The only place—as far as football went—where I could make any kind of honest statement about anything was right out there on the field.

It was early March, training camp was still months away, and I frankly didn't know what being back in New York would be like. But I looked forward to playing now. I wanted to knock some dick loose.

19

IVERY and I both knew at the same time that I was done with rehabilitation. The way we figured it out was by getting in a screaming argument with each other. What started out as a search for a lost ball in some fairway rough ended up with each of us telling the other he had had it. After I left the hospital, we had been in each other's company every minute of every day for six weeks. If one guy—say, me—is the type who never closes a door, picks up a sock, cooks a meal, or washes a dish, and the other is a type who knows how to read French wine labels and knows where everything goes, then you can count on trouble.

But in this case, trouble was sweet.

"I'm sick and tired of seeing your damned face!"

"Your face is no bargain, either."

"That's fine. Maybe it's time for me to go home."

"You go whenever you like."

I felt strong enough to leave Ivery right then. I felt that way when I cooled off, too. Each day, each hour I didn't use drugs, the need for them decreased, too. I reached a point— I'm not even sure when it was—that I could tell myself, "I've gone this far, maybe now I can go some on my own." I knew that my blood was free—something I needed to know. Was my mind free? From the time I spent with Dr. Murabe, I knew that my problems couldn't be reduced to crystals and powders. They had to do with people—with feelings and needs.

What I had to find out now could only come from living with my family, really being free again, in a world where I had to make responsible choices.

This had been no "rehabilitation" to put in the text-books. I cooled out, same as I would have in any detox tank. But that's when the train switched tracks. I followed my own impulses, doing things I wanted to do—like play golf—from day to day. AA and the halfway houses, all the places that have well-meaning programs and plans, were impossible for me. I don't know what I might have gotten out of them, but I know I spent my time not thinking of myself as a sick person but as one who was alive and well. I didn't go through this process where I was trained to think of myself as afflicted and burdened; just the opposite. I enjoyed myself and got free of the pressure cooker that was New York for a while. I never wound up feeling that a part of my brain—the wild part—had been removed or neutralized so that I might get on with my life, trouble-free but cowlike.

When I came back to my family, I honestly didn't know if what I had been through had really worked. You can't ever know something like that anyway. It all has to do with the future, and the future, as any detox program—and anyone with common sense—tells you, really does go by one day at a time. Even as I write this, the days pass just the same.

I've been asked too many times about what I've been through and about what advice I have to give to people. I have none because I don't know if my experience is valid for anyone else. Who am I to tell anyone what they should or shouldn't do? I go to schools, and educators and parents want me to know that I'm a role model for their children, that I have a great deal to say that might help kids who are in trouble.

Damn.

I tell them, you are the role models, especially you parents. Don't put it off on people you don't even know. You think you know me because I'm an image on the TV and in the papers? I'm not who you think I am, and I can never be anyone else's dream.

But surely, I'm told, you can speak out against drugs, you can help people see that it's wrong and that it will waste your life.

I can't even really do that, because I just don't know enough to tell anyone anything. I did this recovery my way—no one else's—and that's all I can speak to. I'm off drugs because I want to be, because the people I love matter to me. There's a whole lot of hypocrisy and bullshit out there about drugs and, because of it, people who want and need to get help may not find it so easily.

I'm an athlete, not a politician or a cop. Athletes these days are especially singled out when the drug problem comes up, even though drugs pervade the whole society and matter a hell of a lot more when they're used by people flying planes, or operating on brains, or sitting in bunkers with their fingers on little missile buttons.

I begin with the basics here. Are drugs wrong? They're illegal, you can say that. That means that if you're smart, you shouldn't use them. But are they wrong? I've never answered questions about right or wrong on the basis of other people making laws about something. The law in South Africa says that apartheid is okay.

I know that drugs are wrong for me because they started to control me and in controlling me they took me away from the people I love and care about most in the world. But I don't even know if that would be the case for everyone else. It may be that drugs sometimes help people relax when nothing else does. Hell, doctors prescribe drugs all the time for just that purpose.

I tell you what: sometimes I think drugs are illegal because big money keeps it that way. What costs a few cents out of some miserable poppy field costs a fortune out in the streets. Take the money out of drugs and I have a feeling the "problem" would be very different. You wouldn't be talking about crime and law enforcement but who a person is and why he needs—or doesn't need—drugs to get by.

There's something else, too. Depending on who you are, if you get nailed for drugs you won't be seen quite the same way by society. An athlete will get dumped on heavier than an entertainer, a black athlete will get dumped on heavier than both. Here's one for you. Just think of Dwight Gooden and Keith Hernandez, teammates who have both come up with drug problems in their careers. Hernandez, today, can go into a batting slump without anyone batting an eye. Gooden will never enjoy a similar luxury. There are going to be philosophical treatises about his character and his impact on American youth for as long as he wears a baseball uniform.

No, I don't have advice for anyone

A friend of mine recently asked me what I would do if my own son came to me one day and said, "Pop, I'm on drugs." I would tell my son that I wish he wasn't, but that he would have to make his own choices—because nothing matters in anything unless you freely choose what you do. I would tell him about my own experience as best I could, about the hurt it caused me and his mother and him, too. But aside from refusing to support his habit, I would issue no orders and call no cops.

It would break my heart if he hurt himself. But the choice would be his. I would stand with him and love him till the last breath in my body, I would spend every cent I had and travel the world over to help cure him, but I would never try to steal the most precious thing he or anyone else has: the power to choose for himself. I love him that much.

I think people were waiting for me to apologize or to tuck my tail between my legs. That was never going to happen with me. There was no way I could kiss ass and still live with myself. If I did that—if I got out there and said how I'd seen the light and how writers like Hank Gola, Dave Klein, and Paul Zimmerman were right all along, I not only would have been lying but I would probably have gone under before I ever got out. That I'm a free spirit, that I control my own fate, that I make all the decisions concerning me is what keeps me going. I just can't live any other way.

When I got home, I had even fewer answers than I do now. I had a game plan—which was just to play football as well as I could—and keep my mouth shut. My insides were drawn tight as a bow. I didn't know what to expect—other than a pile of questions from the media that, I knew in advance, I wasn't going to answer.

I went to a friend's wedding shortly after I got back to New York. It was really the first time I was out in public since I had been in rehab. I remember sitting through this service in church and saying to Paul and Linda, "Man, this is long. When is it going to be over?" I felt jumpy as a cat in public.

I went to my friend's reception afterward. There were a couple of thousand people there; a lot of folks let me know they wished me well. But the main thing was they didn't crowd around. My friend's family saw to that—and so after a while, I could get out on the floor and dance. Just that. And at the time, it seemed like enough.

In training camp, which opened later in the summer, there seemed to be no way to avoid the press. And I mean they were into this drug thing as though I had never played five years in the pros. I went to a charity golf tournament one day and got lost trying to find my way to the course. Next day, one of my favorite New York papers had a picture of me with a golf club in my hands. The caption was IRONING OUT HIS PROBLEMS?

Bill Parcells stepped in at that point—at the beginning of training camp—and made it possible for me to have a season. He told the media that if they didn't leave me alone, that if they came on with any more personal stuff about me, he would close the damn locker room to them for the season.

I will always be grateful to Bill for that. He made it possible for me to get back to football, to just try and concentrate on what I had to do for the season. With no interviews to worry about, there was only football.

At camp, people were all over the place reaching out to me, fans, writers, well-wishers. I appreciated that—but I was plenty on guard, too.

"LT, how're ya doin'?"

"I'm doin' fine. How're you doin'?"

In 1986 the season just happened to open with Dallas. Survival from the opening kickoff of the year. You always walk into Dallas with your eyes open and a game plan in your head. It's funny when I think about it now; like the Super Bowl, my plan for that game was to come in at low weight, speed weight. Dallas, like Denver, comes at you with finesse. Dallas's offensive tackle, Phil Pozderac, is mammoth, but the thing about him is that he has quick feet, just the kind of sonuvabitch who'll give me fits. I knew I wasn't going to be able to bull-rush him, I had to do it with speed. I didn't eat for two days befoe the game, and I dropped my ten pounds.

And just like Pasadena, I was a little surprised by the heat.

In the first half, we were slow and sluggish but we managed to get back in a game that might have gotten out of hand. We were down, 17–14, at the half after spotting the Cowboys two touchdowns early. But Dallas surprised the hell out of us in the second half. They came out and played intensely physical football. It was very uncharacteristic, and it got to us. By the fourth quarter, after we had moved out in front of them, 28–24, they started moving the ball—with only a couple of minutes left.

There were really two big parts to this Dallas drive. One

was a big ole pass play to Tony Hill from somewhere in their territory to our sixteen-yard line. The other was damn fatigue. We got tired; I got tired. I just plain got tired in that game. I knew on a few plays I could have hustled more. We were all back there now and I'm looking at the damn clock and I'm feeling like some boxer who's just had his bell rung but still has two minutes to go before the round is over. I don't know whether it was the humidity, the lateness of the game, the punishing way Dallas was playing, or what, but I was dazed and tired and praying to God the sonsuvbitches would call a time-out. They didn't. Instead, they lined up.

I saw Doug Cosbie come out on the slot opposite me, and I saw that he had a funny look in his eye.

"Why the fuck is he looking at me like that?" I wondered. If I was alert, I sure would have known why. I would have been able to read run. Because that was what was coming. I mean, Cosbie doesn't line up like that—but by the time my tired brain said "run," it was too late. I was on the ground on the bottom of a pile of bodies, and there's Herschel Walker sailing over the top. I hated to see him score—but there he went, All-World, streaking overhead like some silver bomber. Fuck him.

Just then I saw another face on the bottom of the pile. It was Harry. He was as flat on his ass as I was. We just looked at each other as Herschel went sailing into the end zone. We both said, almost simultaneously—both of us in this high-pitched falsetto as we got to our feet: *"Daaaaammmmmnnn!"*

We both knew we had lost the game. But for me, it was a relief because I was only thinking about getting my breath back. When I get too hot and out of breath and we're backed up, I sometimes get like that. Five yards at a time is like torture. It's either score or put me out of my misery. Nobody's a hero when they're just too tired.

I also knew that in a few minutes we'd be back in the dressing room and that all the old questions would be starting up again. I didn't want the season to start this way, but what the hell could you do about it? For sure, I wasn't going to put on for anyone. It pissed me off not to win. And, as before, I wasn't going to talk to anyone about it.

I knew that I had to do it on the field, do it till it's so obvious no one can say a damned thing. And I hadn't done it in Dallas.

Damn. Damn. Damn.

In earlier years, it would have been just another loss; not now. I mean, I just knew what was coming, if not right then, then soon.

A couple of weeks later, it came. We had beaten the Raiders in Los Angeles, 14–9, but I was out of it in that game, too. I had an impacted tooth that bothered me during the week, to the point where I had tried to cut the bad boy out of my mouth on my own. I wound up in the hospital for an afternoon and I was on antibiotics and feeling woozy on game day.

That was it. Two and two equal you-know-what.

When *Sports Illustrated* came out the next week, I was on the cover with Mark Gastineau. The story inside, about the Giants and Jets, had this little number about me: "Giants linebacker Lawrence Taylor boycotts the press, but there's not much to write about anyway. He seems to poop out toward the end of games."

It was certainly true that I wasn't talking to the press. But I tell you what. If I was supposed to, this wasn't about to make me do it. Just the opposite. I stayed away from the press not because I hate them; I don't. They have their job to do. And I have mine. My job at that point was just to play the game.

I was playing for my life.

It just so happened that this little greeting card in *SI* was something I remembered in the weeks that followed.

I didn't ever have to try harder, because my game had never changed. It was always built on being wild and aban-doned. But every time I body-slammed some poor sonuvabitch in the weeks that followed, I found myself saying, "Not much to write about, huh?"

If it was going to be a war out there, my side wasn't about to get defeated.

Maybe that was the whole point.

It was just that I—and no one else on the New York Giants—ever thought about the Super Bowl back in September and October. The war then was strictly personal. It couldn't have been any other way.

20

FOR the first few weeks of the 1986 season, I stayed home nearly all the time. Going to practice was like going to the office. I felt more like a banker than a ballplayer. I did my job, I watched film, and I watched my ass. I was clean as a whistle. And I hated the way I played football.

Sometime around the fourth week of the season, I started going out again. I hit a few bars, had some drinks, and sometimes got home late enough so that Linda and I would fight about it. Before the second Washington game of the season—when we won, 24–14, down at RFK and got an inside track to the NFC Eastern Division title—we got into a real bad one. Linda wouldn't talk to me for two days before the game. When I left home to join the team for our trip, she finally broke her silence.

"Have a good game," she said. Nothing more. I did. I had one of my best. And I did because I was in a rage. You can't fake that. You are or you aren't. There's no switch you can throw. I took out all the anger, fear, and frustration I was feeling that week on Jay Schroeder. I tattooed his ass. Joe Jacoby, the Redskins' 6-7, 305-pound All-Pro left tackle was just another street corner where you made a left turn.

For me, crazy as it seems, there is a real relationship between being wild, reckless, and abandoned off the field and being that way on the field. I believe that when the day comes when I sit home in my slippers watching the paint dry, that will be the day my powers will be gone on a football field. That day may be coming . . . but not yet.

If I hadn't been coming off rehab, this might not even be worth talking about. But being a wild man with my past made it something else. One night, I went to a local tavern to do a little promotional gig. I drank too much, joked around too much, posed for too many pictures, and thought it would be just fine to hang out afterward with a bunch of people I knew I would never see again. We had gotten into a car and one of the people took out a little plastic bag. There was white powder in it.

Before anyone could offer me anything, I said, "This game's too fast for me," and was out of the car. I did know about *that*. The edge is a line you can live close to, but only if you know what's on the other side.

I dragged my ass through the first weeks of the season because I didn't know what to expect from myself. Johnny Parker, our weight coach, made a big point of telling the media at Pasadena last January that he thought I might be a much stronger, quicker player if I regularly lifted weights. The thing was, in the beginning of the season, I did. But I hated it—as I had in the past. Like all the other parts of the game that involve boring repetition, I wound up feeling boring and repetitious as a football player. I told Coach Parker at the end of the season, "Hey, show me one guy in your program who's been to the Pro Bowl six times, who's been named Player of the Year, MVP, and Defensive Player of the Year, and I'll join your program for keeps."

That may make me sound like a real asshole. But I've made my way as a football player by free-lancing.

That's what keeps me at the level I'm at. Something happens to me when I try to do things by the numbers. I want to avoid it every time. Doing things my way isn't just a matter of pride or stubbornness, it's a matter of energy. Something gets switched on when I'm free to do what I want. Something gets switched off when I try to do it by rote. That is a football statement every bit as much as a personal one.

I need to be free to follow this energy or this feeling or whatever you want to call it. Something will happen to me at the line of scrimmage, I won't have time to figure out what it is or why it happened, but I will follow it even if it means deliberately breaking a coverage call or a blocking assignment. Technique has helped me along the way, but this invisible other thing has gotten me all the way from Lightfoot to maybe one day hanging number 56 in the Hall of Fame.

I seem to get to this energy by following the wildness that's inside of me rather than the rule book or playbook. If I don't come into a game with my eyes red, my ears pinned back, and hell in my heart, I'd be just another number in a football suit.

Sometimes guilt for the way I've been earlier in the week gets me fired up for Sundays. Linda doesn't understand that one, and I'm not sure I do, either. Sometimes it's just the rush of the wildness itself, the speeding from Tuesday right on through game day. There was a time when I partied extra hard before a game and would make it a special point of coming out there extra hard for the game—as though to prove to the guys that no one was crazier than I was. In reality I was just keeping continuity with what I had gotten going during the week. Like music, keeping the beat.

But last season could never be like that. Because of what I had been through, I not only could feel a hundred thousand cold eyes on me, I now could feel my own—watching and waiting. I was a person who had been to hell and back, carrying the people I love there with me, and I could never be quite the same again. But my game depended on this mental edge, and to keep it was something like walking a tightrope.

In the seventh game of the season, we went out to Seattle and got beaten in the Kingdome, 17–12. It was the last game we were to lose all season, but at the time I remember being convinced there would be several others to follow. I was frustrated because I had been shut down. The Seahawks had run all kinds of misdirection plays at me, and I somehow had gone for them all. At the end of the game, I had felt that my head had been thoroughly messed with. But I was even more pissed off by what I had seen around me. We had any number of opportunities to win the game, but the damn offense couldn't do the job. Oh, yeah, we had been through that one before.

I remember after that Seattle game sitting with a friend and unloading all these nasty nagging feelings I had had for years. Our offensive coordinator, I said, was a real nice guy but a dick—no imagination, everything predictable. That wasn't true—as the rest of our season proved—but I said it. I said our quarterback was a semi-dick: I mean, Phil was a quarterback who somehow just didn't see the field. It was like he got this fixed idea in his head about who he was going to throw to and then didn't see this or that other receiver who was wide open. He held the ball too damn long, he took more sacks than he had any reason to, he didn't know how to throw the ball away, he was a guy who was constantly looking for the home run. Because he had a great arm and was a real competitor, sometimes he'd lead us, but sometimes he wouldn't. I wasn't much different from Giant fans everywhere.

I told my friend what I and a lot of other players had talked about among ourselves for a long time—that if Bill wasn't hampered by so much loyalty to his players, he'd let Jeff Rutledge take the quarterback job. There were a lot of us who believed then that Jeff could move the team better than Phil.

Our wide receivers, I told my friend, weren't really able to do the job. Lionel Manuel was the only speed burner we had, and he had been injured weeks before and was out for the season. Our offensive line had guys who were good athletes but were missing some spark or other. In place after place, we had good—but not great—personnel. On teams that went to the Super Bowl—this was my big point—there was always the ability for one part of the squad to make up for a temporary letdown by the other. If the defense played poorly, the offense would pick you up—and vice versa. If the running game was closed down, then the passing game would be there. The Giants, I told my friend, couldn't compensate in this way. If you closed down the passing game or if we had to play catch-up against a good team, that would be it for us.

We didn't lose a game after that!

I was pissed—that was all. My anger and frustration got the best of my judgment.

But there was something else there, too. That was really the first time that season my thoughts went past myself, to the team. I had been so intent on just making sure I played well that I hadn't spent much time looking at the team around me. As we started to win, I felt more comfortable. We followed the Seattle loss with two big wins at home against Dallas and Washington and then began a stretch of five games, four on the road, all against tough teams. We won all those and everything else after that right through the Super Bowl.

There's nothing like winning to help you see what's around you.

We were a young team; there were only a handful of older players. In '83, '85, and '86, we had big draft years, and there were suddenly guys just starting to come into their own who really could play ball. We *did* have a running game. When Joe Morris came up, you couldn't see that right away. He was—and is—a quiet guy who kept to himself a lot. He had a tendency to trip over his own feet. He didn't play much right away, and it was kind of a surprise to everybody—except maybe to him—when he found his feet in 1985. But he was one hell of a ballcarrier for us then, and once he got past that contract holdout from the summer, he was primed for '86. What no one realized was that Joe has this thing pushing him—with me it's wildness, with him I think it's his size. I think he has a short man's psychology. You say no to Joe, he'll come at you twice as hard till you say yes, then he'll come at you three times as hard.

Mark Bavaro, the super quiet one, came in '85. Zeke Mowatt was our number one tight end then, but when an injury took him out, Mark turned out to be a horse. Well, he was a horse from the start. I remember in his first summer camp, we started going at it, really blocking and hitting the shit out of each other. It was a challenge—and let me tell you, he didn't give an inch. We made a truce, the way Leon Perry and I once had: "Hey, man, we don't need to be doing this," I told Mark. He just nodded.

Mark's quietness is the real thing. Our GM, George Young, says that Bavaro's priest had coaxed him into talking by getting him to read from Scripture—that was how the priest found out Mark had a Massachusetts accent. I still don't know what kind of accent he has. To this day, when he walks up to me and asks me a question, I go into shock. New Year's Eve, the season before last, I had a party at my house. The doorbell rang. I answered it and it was Mark—dressed very neatly in a suit—with his girlfriend. I nearly fell over with surprise to see him there. The guy's no surprise out on the field, though. I *know*—my own body has the bruises to show for it—why he is able to drag four tacklers halfway down a football field. Mark is also a health-food freak and the only guy I've ever met whose locker is a bigger mess than mine.

Phil Simms, too, even though he's thirty, is really young in terms of his playing time. Last season was only the third one he's had free of injury. If you watched the Minnesota game—which we won in the last seconds on a field goal after Phil made a great fourth-down play to keep our final drive going—you would have seen what a lot us, including every guy who ever criticized Phil, knew perfectly well. Contrary to what a lot of fans said, he was a guy who could lead a team. He had the guts of a riverboat gambler and the ability to come right back after a bad game.

Phil, like Parcells and myself, is a guy who will bet you on anything and everything. We're always at cards on our road trips, and Phil wants to beat you as badly as I do—or as anyone else you'll run into. What happened to Phil in the Seattle game wasn't really so hard to figure. He had a bad game. He was off. He was aiming the ball instead of throwing it. He lost his confidence.

Bill told him to go out there and forget about trying to be cute or worrying about interceptions, to just let it fly, take chances, be the tough sonuvabitch he really was.

That's what you saw Phil do right through the Super Bowl. Everybody out there, including some of us, just kept underestimating him, and he just kept putting big games on the board one after the other. Nobody's going to underestimate Phil again. You can guess what we might have done with someone else at quarterback last season. There are no guesses with Phil. He led us to the Super Bowl.

I was mercifully glad just to have the chance to play. I think Bill did as much for me last season as any person could have—and I will be grateful to him for that for as long as I live. By keeping the media away from me, he did two things. He took a whole shit pile of pressure off my shoulders, allowing me to concentrate on football—and he put that pressure on his own shoulders. He did something else, too. He let me play my game. He did that in ways fans might not have understood.

I happened to have a statistically great year. I don't think of it as my best. I injured my shoulder in the first Washington game of the season and never got real strength back in it the rest of the way. I missed chances I might have made—like that first Denver game, where I had John Elway sacked three different times but couldn't use my right arm to either wrap him or ax him. Bill kept rushing me, giving me chances to look good at what I do best. He didn't have to. Bill could have made me look much more invisible out there by simply calling plays that dropped me in coverage. He rushed me far more last season than he did in any of my previous seasons with him.

I think Bill knew what letting me concentrate on football meant. He knew what it meant to me personally—and he knew what it meant to the team to have me out there full tilt. The other side of being a "players' coach" is that you have a talent for getting the best out of the personnel you have. Bill has taken a lot of shit from me over the years but has stood by me. I can't change who I am, but I can tip my hat to him. He's my coach and my friend.

Last season, from game to game, from week to week we got better as a team. Harry Carson and Carl Banks both said to the media that our playoff loss to the Bears the year before got us motivated this year because we all knew we were a better team than Chicago. I never felt that. In '85, I thought that if we had played the Bears ten times, they would have beaten us eight out of the ten. (I had another problem in that Bears game. I got distracted—something you never want to happen. Mike Ditka had been riding my ass all day from the sidelines about being a dirty player. I started yelling back at him. And then he had a few plays run at me. Dennis McKinnon caught me in the earhole on one play and knocked the shit out of me. I tried to break him in two on the next play. Then Matt Suey and I got into it, I kept screaming at Ditka, "Bring all the shit you can over to my side." I couldn't have been more out of it if I had been on the moon.) We got better this year—all of us—because we kept winning. Winning, like losing, changes you. For me, personally, winning had nothing magical about it—but it was like a gift I never counted on, coming at a time when all I wanted to do was play ball.

I remember before the second Washington game having this sense of dread that we were going to beat Washington down at RFK but then lose to them in the NFC championship game. I know all the stuff about teams not being able to beat other teams three times in one season, but that was only part of my thinking. The big part, the part I never talked about with anyone, was that I have this pessimistic side. Super athletes aren't supposed to have that. I do. There's a part of me that believes the worst will happen. It's not fear. It's more like a sense of fate—just as I believed on the positive side that the name of the year's Super Bowl winner was written down in advance.

But by playing and winning game after game, I got used to winning with the Giants—something that had never happened before.

When I came to the Giants, I was expected to do it all. I kept hearing how I was the team to the point where I had that expectation from myself, even though I knew that was impossible. I went out last season with more pressure than I've ever played with. A lot of fans, a lot of people in the media still had that same expectation of me, maybe out of habit.

I remember during our Monday night game against the Redskins in October, some people in Giants Stadium held up a big banner that read, "LT is God."

It embarrassed the hell out of me.

For years, I'd been almost paranoid about the look people would get on their faces when I walked through a parking lot or a restaurant—I could never be what I saw in people's eyes as they came toward me. No human being could. Jesus Christ retired a long time ago, and he never played football.

I had a year for myself. I played well, but I don't know if I deserved all the awards I got. Maybe some of them happened because people didn't really think I would come back the way I did and I surprised them. I don't think of last year as my best year. Winning the Super Bowl was something else. And that happened not because I was God but because I was only one of the Blue. One, not all. Last season I was part of a team that grew up as it went along. That was reward in itself.

I can't dissect it as a coach or a media expert would. But I can tell you something about it from a position a few feet from the edge.

I can tell you a little something about the Giant D.

T H E Giants' basic philosophy of defense is this: Kick the shit out of them. What we do is easy to put into words but a little harder to carry out because everything depends on execution. That's why you can go to sleep in a meeting room but still be front and center on Sundays.

From the time I got to the Giants till the present, there has always been a great deal of pride on defense. We pride ourselves on a few simple things—on the way we hit people, putting a lot of pressure on the quarterback, hustling all the time; the last play of the game, whether it's a blowout or a cliff-hanger, you run with the same intensity. We run to the ball—which means that wherever that sonuvabitch bounces, is carried, or is thrown, you're going to see a bunch of blue jerseys there ready to put you through the trash compactor.

We play a lot of zone and will go man-to-man only in special situations or if we're backed up inside our twenty. We don't stunt a lot, we don't try to fool you; when we get you thinking it's mainly about getting hit by someone who's 250 pounds and can do the forty in 4.6. Our game is fundamentals—blocking and tackling and getting to the football. If you get away from that, it doesn't matter if your defense is high-tech or Mile-High, you're going to lose.

The Giants' defense perfectly suited my type of game. Even as a rookie, when I didn't know many of the plays, what I did matched rather than conflicted with what the Giants were after on defense. It's true that back then, playing with reckless abandon, giving 110 percent, jumping and diving onto people, fired up other players around me and the fans, too. Today you're going to see a lot of other players out there on the Giant D who can do big and instant damage. When teams run the ball away from me, they have to go to Carl Banks's side. Don't do that. Carl is so ugly that Bill Parcells warned children not to look at him on morning TV, but he's very bright and sweet—off the field. No one but *no one* in the league plays the run better than he does. This guy gets through blockers like he's invisible and then hits you like a truck or a crazed rhino. With any other team, he would have gone straight to the Pro Bowl last season.

Leonard Marshall is 6-3 and 285 pounds. He looks fat and slow. He's mean and quick. When he and I run a game or a stunt to adjust to a blocking pattern coming at us, one of us is likely to get there.

Jimmy Burt coming up the middle and Harry Carson stuffing the inside can just take the air out of an offense. There's no oxygen left on the line of scrimmage. If you're a quarterback, even if you drop shallow and release the ball quickly, you're liable to get your brains scrambled. We put five quarterbacks on the shelf last year—and it was all clean. All the while we had guys waiting to get in the game who would start for most other teams in the league.

Teams are defined by their linebackers. All units on a team have a special character—your defensive backs, for example, are most often very high-strung and nervous. These little fly guys, the real fast ones, are going to talk all kinds of menace during the week. They tell you who they're going to hit and then they tell you all about their girls and then as game day approaches they get quieter and quieter because they suddenly feel it's on the line for them. Your linemen—defensive and offensive—hang out with each other. They're all big blocky guys and they are the mellow ones on a team; they tend to be shy and easygoing.

The linebackers, because they tend to fall somewhere in the middle—they're linemen *and* defensive backs at the same time—are harder to figure, but when you do, you'll get to the personality of your team. Show me a team's linebackers and I'll tell you a lot about that team's character.

Our linebackers have all tended to be big, fast, and slightly crazy. The Giants like to say that you have to be 6-3 and 230 pounds even to be drafted as a linebacker in the organization, but don't be fooled by anything you hear that sounds just technical. They're looking at what's inside these bodies, too. They won't quite say it, but they're looking for a mind-set in a linebacker that knows hitting is almost as much fun as sex. When I was drafted, I don't think anyone was concerned with how fast or how well I'd take to the playbook. My size, speed, and wildness were *football* qualities the Giants understood. Not that the Giants are looking for people who'll go nuts off the field—it's just that they want guys who have this thing about hitting. All teams talk about it, of course, but the Giants seem to know how to go out there and find it.

There's something about hitting a person, getting in a hard lick, that just turns people on. It gets a crowd going and and it gets your teammates going. I know that I built my career on that, and I still love it. In the early days, when the Giants weren't doing much, I felt extra pressure to come up with one of these plays. On defense it was the equivalent of going for the bomb or the long ball. I got a reputation as a big-play player, but even if you get people fired up, you need something more to win.

Let me tell you about the "big play." It's mainly bullshit. I've always known that, just as I've always known that the "big play" does more to get you noticed than how well you play. Sixty or 70 percent of the time, the defense doesn't do it—the offense simply stops itself. There are three or four times in a game, in specific situations, when a big play counts—and you hope you can be there for it. There are a lot of other times, however, when a big play isn't really big at all, just eye-catching.

Take the business of sacks. A sack gets a crowd jumping out of their seats. You lead the charge. You leap to your feet and everybody is into high-fiving and doing little special numbers. That's fun, although there's a "Gastineau rule" now that cuts down on sack dancing. The thing is *where* a sack comes in a game. It's one thing in a close game when you stop a drive with it; it's another when the game is already decided. If you want to find out what kind of hitting a player is really doing, don't just look for his sack total. See how many tackles he makes. We have sack artists on our club who don't make too many tackles. The year Mark Gastineau set the NFL sack record for one year—he made twenty-two—he had only twenty-something tackles to go with it. I take as much pride in the number and kind of tackles I make as the sacks I get. I take equal pride in seeing offenses going out of sync because of the pressure I bring. But don't kid yourself, sacks mean money; tackles and all the intangibles you can do on defense don't.

Big plays lead to big reputations.

Last season I had more sacks than I ever had in any single season in college or the pros. I came within two of setting an NFL record. I wanted to get it badly in the last two games of the season, but I didn't. The important thing, though, was that in the several games where I didn't make big plays, where the offense worked like good defenses in stopping me, it didn't matter. Last season proved, if anyone needed proof, that stopping me didn't mean you stopped us.

Our philosophy on defense I'm sure came right out of our losing years. When we didn't have the talent we have now, doing things fundamentally and simply were absolutely necessary. We came into last season knowing we were good but never guessing where we would wind up. We had the attitude we always had—that we had to work for everything we got.

We didn't walk out on the field like those old dynasty teams—expecting rather than hoping to win. Our job was to play hard, to execute—stick to basics. It influenced everything we did.

When we played San Diego in the second game of the season, the Chargers had just come off a game where they had scored fifty points. Everyone said they had the league's most high-powered offense. We respected that, of course, but the way we looked at that team—and others like them that used a multiple number of sets and a lot of trick plays—was right out of our "philosophy."

We didn't bite for their multiple sets and formations. Our idea was simple. Wherever one of their players lined up on the field, that's the position he was in. If they lined up with three backs and one of them moved out of the backfield, treat him as a wide receiver. That's the position he's taking. You don't put a linebacker on him, you use one of your corners or safeties to cover him. You don't let them take you out of your game.

The week before, Miami fell for all of that junk—and they got demolished. We didn't stop Dan Fouts with a lot of big sacks. His drop and release were too quick for that. We stuffed the Chargers' run—we did that to every team—and we forced him to throw the ball against constant pressure. We beat them, 20–7, and held them to 265 yards' total offense.

Bill called us a blue-collar team through the year. That wasn't because of our salaries but because of our approach to what we had to do. None of us ever could rest on our laurels. If we won a game in week two, there was week three ahead of us. When we destroyed San Francisco, 49–3, in the playoffs, we didn't celebrate much. Our attitude was that we had the NFC championship game ahead of us. When we won that one, too, we weren't going to be fooled into thinking the Super Bowl was ours before we played it. We thought about the Super Bowl only after we won the NFC championship; we won the Super Bowl only after we went out there and played the game.

Seattle had to have been the low point in the season for us, just as the Super Bowl was the high point. But between the low point and the high point there was no turning point, just winning football games one after the other. It was the winning—not any one play, not any one game—that eventually made us a very different team at the end of the year from the one we were at the beginning.

I think our schedule helped us as much as anything. I don't know what the ranking was, but I can't believe any team had a tougher run of games than we did. We played the Chargers when they were still everybody's favorite offense; we played the Raiders in L.A. when everyone knew they would be extra mean and nasty because they had lost their first two games; we played the Saints, supposedly a "softer" team, and had to come back from 17–0 to beat them; we got the Eagles right at the point where all the writers were saying Buddy Ryan had finally kicked his Bear 46 into gear, and then beginning with the Minnesota game, we hit four games in a row against the Vikings, Broncos, 49ers, and Redskins— three away from home—that could just as easily have put us out of instead of into the championship picture.

There was no time ever to stop and think how good we were. There was only next week.

I didn't get my second sack till the fifth game of the season—against St. Louis. By then, I was feeling much more like my old self. I was off film and out on the town, enjoying myself. I had to make compromises, of course, but I was myself again. I did what I wanted. If I wanted to drink, I drank. If I wanted to go out, I went out.

Most of all, I was who I was on the football field. I didn't change my approach to the game or to authority. I liked it when they called me crazy in 1981; I liked it just as much in 1987. I was no more a hero about practices and preparation than I ever had been. I quit doing weights, I'd go to sleep if a meeting got boring, I'd gun my car around, but I was there on Sundays. And oh yeah, there was no dope.

My recovery was no recovery if I couldn't be myself.

I was pumped by every sack, every hit. Every game had this extraordinary personal pressure to keep it up, to be as good or better than before. There was no great fun in that. But the season happened to carry all of us beyond anything personal we were playing for.

The three Washington games illustrate perfectly what happened to me and to us. The Redskins needed no advance billing when they came into Giants Stadium at the end of October. We were in a game for first place in the East.

I happen to love playing the Redskins. They're physical, the way we are. They play very hard and clean and they don't mess with your head. When we play them, it's eleven guys against eleven guys and the stronger will survive. I love beating them.

The Redskins don't necessarily do the same things from week to week. They may have a tight end in the backfield one week but not another, they may put two tight ends together or split their backs out. But you know that whatever look they give you, they are always going to come at you with their same plays. They're going to run their sweeps, their specials, they'll run their play-action, they'll go short yardage on first down to set up a second and three or four so that they'll be able to bring the full range of their offense into play as soon as possible. In the end, they're not fancy, and neither are we.

But to defense against them, you've got to keep certain things in mind. Washington runs a one-back offense. We know that George Rogers and Kelvin Bryant are not going to wind up blocking for each other, so our setup is designed to take their one-back run and close it down. We have a play—

Down Fire Lion Zero—which is basically keying me to George Rogers. I go where he goes. He almost never gets outside. When they run their special, with their line all pulling one way, we will kick the guard or tackle back inside if we can and penetrate a gap. If George is forced back inside by closing the corner to him, he's dead; if he goes outside, I'm going to devour him. We took Washington's run away in that game and pretty nearly every game we've played them recently because bull to bull, we just beat them.

In that first game, we had a real problem with Jay Schroeder. Schroeder, who was the NFC's Pro Bowl quarterback last season, is big and mobile. He's been the quarterback only a short while—since Joe Theismann broke his leg and had to retire in 1985—but he's given them a dimension they didn't have with Joe. He can move.

We had Jay and the Redskins pretty well contained during the first half. We led, 13–3, going into the locker room, and then when we added another score shortly into the third period, we seemed to be in pretty good shape. That's when Schroeder took over. He rolled up over four hundred passing yards for the game, and most of them seemed to come in the second half. We broke a 20–20 tie with a last-minute touchdown run by Joe Morris.

Now, when a guy rolls up four hundred yards passing on you, there are two possibilities: either he's that good or you're that bad. In our case, it was a combination of both. I knew I was myself in that game for a few reasons. I got some good hits in it, I left the field with my body hurting—I don't know where or how, but my shoulder was on fire—and I was in a rage at the noncoverage we had thrown at Washington. Schroeder had been bombing us for thirty minutes, and whatever we were doing up front to pressure him—we sacked the sonuvadog four times—didn't seem to matter. One of our defensive backs fell down on one long pass; there were stupid calls and blown coverages on others. I went crazy.

I hollered at the defensive backs for making the same mistakes twice, I hollered at our coaches for calling the same plays that had gotten us burned just before. I wound up kicking over some Gatorade—sorry, Bill and Harry—and being just a madman on the sideline.

I was back.

In the second Washington game, we didn't prepare much differently than for the first game. We knew who we were playing, and we knew the stakes. Whoever won this second game, at RFK in December, was going to wind up as Eastern Division champion and get home field for the play-offs. It didn't take an expert to tell any of us that we couldn't let Schroeder do to us this time what he did in the first game.

I didn't watch film, I didn't pay that much attention during the meetings. As long as I knew Washington wasn't coming at us with something brand-new, I just wanted to play the game. The fight I was having with Linda that week did more for me than the meetings and practices.

We all wanted to close down Schroeder. We all knew that as big and mobile as he was, he ran basically to find throwing room—not, like John Elway, also to look for rushing yards. We wanted to keep him in the pocket if we could, but we also wanted to pressure him wherever he was. For me, the best pressure would be to cream him. I'll take a hurry-up, anything that helps, but if I can demolish a guy, that's the best. Nothing takes the heart out of you faster than having a safe fall on your head when you're not looking.

I *wanted* Jay Schroeder. And I got him. I hit him blind side, onside, and upside down. I was in his face again and again. I sacked him three times and was near him all afternoon. It was one of those games where I just was not going to be denied. I had no problem beating Joe Jacoby or anyone else. Nothing seemed to get in the way—not even our own play calling. On two of the sacks I got, my assignment was to drop in coverage. Sometimes you go by the book and you're going to lose. Try to tell that to a coach. I don't. I just do what I have to.

The championship game was as different from the second Washington game as the second was from the first. The Redskins, like any good team, aren't going to get beat the same way twice. Like a lot of teams had late in the year, they seemed determined to make sure they weren't going to let me be a factor. I was double-teamed, triple-teamed, and just plain worked over all afternoon as we shut out the Skins for the title, 17–0.

I was as happy as could be. I played my part simply by making those sonsuvbitches work too hard on me, making them vulnerable elsewhere. The point was that we had other guys ready and able to wreck them.

You want to know about the Giant D? Look at Jay Schroeder through those three games. In the first, the man was a bombardier. In the second, he got his wings shot out from under him. In the championship game, whenever he dropped back to pass, he would suddenly give this little twist of the head to see if anything was coming from his blind side just before he released the ball. He was shell-shocked. He just wasn't the same player he was the first time he faced us. That isn't to say he won't get out there and bomb us silly at some time again, but in 1986, running what we did at him, we hit his body and got to his head.

I had myself a season, all right. But my team gave me a season, too. Toward the end of the year, I made up paper-weights in the shape of Super Bowl rings that I gave to every member of the team. It was my way of saying thanks for making things a little easier in the roughest year of my life. If you want to talk about my comeback, don't forget to talk about the Giant D.

22

NOTHING more perfectly illustrates the unreality of Super Bowl hype than an interview I had a couple of weeks before the game in January 1987.

During the first of these two weeks leading up to the game, a camera crew from one of the networks came to my house along with a guy who was going to do the interview. It took a while setting up, getting the lights placed just right, getting Linda and me seated correctly on the couch, figuring out how to get the kids and our dog, Taffy, into some of the shots.

The interview was nice and warm. The interviewer asked Linda and me about my comeback and about our life together. The questions were personal but general enough to handle easily. I was at ease, Linda was at ease, the interviewer was at ease. The interviewer didn't ask and Linda and I didn't say anything about what we had really been through. It was a Super Bowl story, the way there are Thanksgiving stories and Christmas stories; families everywhere could appreciate it.

The only thing out of focus in this cozy picture is that the interviewer was a neighbor of ours, a drinking and card buddy of mine who knew my story as well as I did—because I had never hidden it from him. He knew I wasn't going to answer any questions about my "problems," but he had a job to do—just as I did. It was Super Bowl time. You talk at Super Bowl time. You feed the hype machine. I was free enough to do that now. My buddy and I fed it together.

Anybody who's ever played professional football dreams about getting to the Super Bowl. There's no bigger award a player can receive. But there should also be an award for surviving the two weeks around it. One part is a game, the rest of it will one day put Walt Disney out of business.

Bill Parcells was smart to keep us back home for the first week. We accomplished as much as we would have in California, but without being prisoners in an overrun hotel. We were free to come and go, sleep in our beds, drive our own cars, think of what we had to do as a continuation of what we had been doing all season rather than as something totally separate. The only difference between that first week and a normal workweek for us was the crowd of media in our locker room. You never saw anything like it. You had more chance of getting killed in that crush than out on the field.

A lot of us ran our own D to survive. Guys hung out in back rooms where the media couldn't go. Tony Galbreath walked around with a videocam doing media on the media; Harry Carson and I, because we had adjoining lockers, did our own little bit. Sometimes we'd interview each other, Harry would start philosophizing, and I'd start mumbling obscenities. Under pressure of a deadline, you'll skip stories like ours.

In California, we stayed in a hotel in Costa Mesa, about an hour out of Los Angeles. If the idea was to keep the crowds away, it sure didn't work. The lobby, the halls, and the parking lots around the hotel were just crawling with people. And you couldn't tell the media from the tourists.

When we came to and from practice, a number of us just couldn't face getting mauled on the way to the elevators. We came in through the back, through the kitchen, and up some rear elevators. We had security on the floors where we stayed, but even that wasn't all that secure. There were all kinds of people with all kinds of stories coming to the security desks, and then there was the telephone. Every time I got to my room, there were at least sixty messages waiting for me. From the moment I walked into the room, the phone kept ringing—until I'd have to put the receiver off the hook. I'd answer the phone, disguising my voice.

"Lawrence Taylor, please?"

"Ay yam sorry. Hee no heer now. Later try."

I'd pinch my nose and squeeze my voice up through my throat. I'm not sure if I sounded like Mickey Mouse or a bad imitation of a guy without a green card. But it didn't do much good.

There were two days reserved for media interviews, Tuesday and Wednesday. One was supposedly for photographers, the other for print. I say supposedly because on photographers' day I got surrounded by a horde of people with cameras, microphones, tape recorders, and note pads. I thought that would take care of it for the week. Fine. I went up into the bleachers, had these media people all around me, and went at it for an hour or so. I kinda liked the pictures that came out next day—I looked like I was holding court.

Unfortunately, that wasn't the end of it. The next day, at nine o'clock in the morning, there was another media call. I didn't want to go to this one, but Bill told me there was some sort of league fine of five thousand bucks for skipping it, and that just seemed like too big a bite; something less than that and I would have gladly paid, but there I was. To make matters worse, I had been out till four the night before, the only time all week I had been able to get away. So I came late to this session, looking mean and nasty, like I had been wasted the night before. I spat tobacco juice on the carpet next to me and basically was an asshole. You can take just so many questions about Denver and dope.

To be a football player, *just* a football player in these

circumstances is all but impossible. You wind up doing things you'd never dream of doing during the season. Some guys, the ones who are not really private people, love it. Guys like Harry, Jimmy, Phil McConkey, Leonard Marshall— all of them great players—just get turned on by this stuff. Then there are guys who have played one game after another in total obscurity, who have never been asked a single question by a single reporter, who now find themselves besieged, answering questions about everything from their sex life to the brand of cups they use.

A lot of guys see all of this as their one chance to make some real money, something I'd never put a football player down for. Jerome Sally and a few other guys were out there trying to hustle a video; you know, we've got to have a Super Bowl Shuffle, too. There were other guys pushing their agents all over Hollywood to hustle the talk shows and studios. Then there was Gary Reasons all by himself trying to hustle a linebackers' poster the day before the biggest game of his life—where we'd all be dressed up in Superman suits, looking mean and indestructible. We were out there for him, too.

For the more private guys it's just as unreal. Most of the time, I stayed in my hotel room. I couldn't sleep, the more it got to me. I think I got a total of fifteen hours of sleep the whole time I was in California. It seemed like I was watching a pay-TV movie, *Top Gun*, over and over again. I liked the movie, it was better than anything on regular TV. I liked the character Tom Cruise played—a guy with authority who bucks authority and who knows he'll have to pay for it in the end. But twelve times! I saw that movie twelve times!

The one night I did get out, there was still no way of getting away from anything. For a week and a half I had been reading and hearing and seeing all this horseshit about how the game would somehow boil down to "LT vs. Elway." All it did was add to the pressure. I knew it wasn't true, but I kept seeing it every day to the point where it was hard to keep it out of my head.

So this one night out, a few of us went to a club called The Red Onion in L.A. And who was there but John Elway and some of the other Bronco players. Three of these guys were judging a hot body contest, and John was just sitting there at a table nearby. Know what I did? I didn't watch the hot body contest, I watched Elway. I sat there with my shades on, staring at him for ten, fifteen solid minutes. It was like a Clint Eastwood movie, and everybody in the place seemed to pick up on it. I mean, it was intense—it was the one chance I had all week to enjoy myself—and it was right out of all that Hollywood make-believe. After a while John came over and we had a good talk.

My nemesis turned out to be a really decent guy, very sincere, someone you knew had come to California for football, not "LT vs. Elway."

As for the football part of the Super Bowl, the practice field was just about the only refuge I had. It wasn't that my attitude to practice suddenly changed, it was just that practice was the only place where I could really enjoy myself.

We trained at the Rams' complex in Anaheim. The first day, there was this little dog there that had been rescued from the pound just hours before he was scheduled to be turned into Taco Bell filling. His name was Ofer—because he had been oh-for-four in life, I guess—and he was just the damndest dog you ever saw. He was playful and smart and turned on to the idea of being a soccer goalie. Whenever you'd kick a tennis ball in his direction, he'd block it. A few of us decided to really give him a try. We set up a goal in the Rams' dressing room and put Ofer out in front of it.

None of us could get a ball past him consistently. That first day, I must have tried fifty times, kicking this small ball as hard as I could—and got no more than five past him. I spent two days figuring out the head and foot fakes to beat him—and finally did. No way a dog is going to beat me. I got down on all fours with Ofer and I played all kinds of games with him—and a few other people. One day I caught Bobby Johnson asleep on the floor in front of his locker—watch out, Bobby. I carefully rolled the ball up onto his chest right under his chin. I knew Ofer well enough by then to know that, like a good defensive player, he always went for the ball.

Speaking of sleeping in meetings, I was able to make a big improvement in technique in California. The morning after I had been to the The Red Onion and gone through round two with the press, I sat down for a linebackers' meeting geared for action. Bill Belichick, our defensive coordinator, passed out some scouting reports on the Broncos. I took mine, a thick batch of papers, and held it up in front of me. I was at a desk where I could lean forward on my elbows, propping the papers up in reading position. I had my shades on so no one could really tell that I wasn't studying hard. I *looked* like I was. I was told later that Bill, at one point, said something like: "Got that, LT?"

He apparently repeated this several times and couldn't figure out why I wasn't answering him. He walked over to me, took the shades off my face, saw that I was sound asleep, and then—here's what I remember—shook my shoulders and said, "Holy shit, you're really sleeping!"

The only way I can see improving on that one would be sleeping with my eyes open. I'm working on it.

It was hard to figure us in practice that week. We didn't get really intense until the Friday before the game. During the entire week before the San Francisco playoff, everyone was wired all the time—I was hell on wheels to be around then. A couple of days before the Washington game, same thing.

But out in California, it was just hard to read. One day, on the bus going to practice, Joe Morris, who normally keeps things to himself, suddenly got off on the strength and conditioning coach, Johnny Parker. It seems that John had been coming down on him for easing up on his weight program. John had told him that the year before, when Joe had a good season, Joe needed him—just as he did at the beginning of this year, when Joe had reported late to camp. Joe teed off. "Man, I didn't need you last year, I didn't need you this year, and I won't need you next year," he said.

I don't know if anyone got upset by that or not; for me, it was a good sign. Jim Burt and I kept teasing Joe all through practice, urging him to defy the coaches: "Join the renegades, Joe, that's it, you can do it. We need you. There's only a few of us left around here."

When we got back to the locker room, Jim and I were still into this one. We walked up and down in front of the lockers, recruiting the renegades. I walked out front; Jim was right behind me.

"Brad Benson? Nah, a conformist. Phil Simms . . . conformist. Erik Howard . . . could be a new addition to the renegades. Phil McConkey . . . conformist." We stopped near Harry's locker. I said, "He used to be a renegade; now, definitely . . . conformist. Elvis? Yeah, he's a renegade, but we don't want him because he doesn't know what he's doing." Then we came to Leonard Marshall. I looked at Jimmy, then at Leonard, and said, "He's not a renegade and he's not a conformist, he's an ass-kisser." I kept moving down the line. Suddenly Leonard flipped out. He started raving and ranting—not at me but at *Jimmy.* No one had the right to call him an ass-kisser, he hollered, and before you knew it he and Jimmy were ready for combat right there—even though it was me, not Jimmy, who had called him an ass-kisser. Crazy. If Bill hadn't come running to break it up, serious damage might have been done.

As far as I was concerned, we were starting to look good. I didn't have the game I wanted to have in the Super

Bowl, but it was the fulfillment of a dream because we won. If we had lost and I had twenty sacks, none of the awards and press clips would have meant a thing. Not with this game.

I had my own routine going in. I knew what our job was, I knew what mine was. The key to stopping Denver obviously was stopping John. John is 6-4 and 215 or 220 pounds, runs the forty in 4.6, and on top of it has that arm. Our plan was not to rush me all the time but to have the ends pinch in on him while I stayed back as a mirror. I would mirror every move of John's and then if we were not able to keep him in the pocket, if he was forced out, I would come up to get him. It was important for us to try to keep John in the pocket because he is such a deadly passer on the run. Jay Schroeder, for example, though he's big and mobile, can't do all that much when he's moving laterally. John can—as he well proved in that first half against us.

When we finally blew Denver out, we had changed very little of what we were doing. We went to more man-to-man coverage, trying to take away the short pass from Elway so he would wind up having to hold on to the ball a little longer. But basically we just picked up our intensity and executed. What everybody saw in the second half was the team we had become over the year. The D was there, and so was our offense. If you want to look at what changed on the Giants over the year, look at our offense. We had been putting points on the board in a big way for quite a while; we were a team that had peaked when we went into the Super Bowl, and it just took playing like ourselves to flatten the Broncos.

I finished that game more tired than I've ever been before. I had my weight down to speed weight—235, the lightest I've ever been in the pros. But as in the first Dallas game, it didn't seem to work. The heat of the day, a lot of sleeplessness, a nagging injury to my thigh, the shoulder injury I had—it came out of its socket during our last full practice on Friday—all wound up making me feel slower rather than faster. When I came to the Rose Bowl that morning, I remember the first thing I did was take a shower—to cool off, to wake up. That wasn't my routine. That was my tired body looking for relief.

I was never as happy as when we won. We were the best—for one year. No one could ever take that away from us. That was beyond hype and beyond fatigue. We were the best for this one year.

I have to be honest and say that I counted the games, then the days, then finally the hours and the minutes to the end of the season. I wanted it over, I wanted it behind me. I can't really rate my seasons, but I know that I had more fun—and I believe I've played better—in other seasons.

Because of the "trouble" I had, people were very generous to me last year, including some people in the media. Many of them were very willing to make the most of every good move I made, to the point where possibly they might have overlooked some things I didn't do. When the Super Bowl ended and we all went back to our sardine can of a dressing room, somebody got me to put on that old red cape and Superman shirt for one last postgame interview. I obliged. I stood there sweating and aching, waiting for it to be over. I was neither Superman nor even enjoying myself in that crush. I wasn't a hero when I walked into the NFL, and I won't be the day I walk out.

What about this year you had, LT? What about that comeback?

No one can take away from me what I did, no one can change it. But there are no awards for the most important part of my season. What I played for was in the hearts of the people I loved, whom I had hurt so deeply. Each week, each game where I did well, the reward was in their eyes and in my sense of just being stronger. I played the game the way I can play it. No one can ever take that away from me. That was my answer, that was the real test this renegade set for himself—and passed. I did it.

Here's a little secret: I was bone tired and hurt not

through one game but through the last four or five games we played. In the San Francisco game, when I intercepted a pass and ran it back for a touchdown, I was thinking on my way to the end zone—just as I had in that Detroit game in '82— "What do I do when I get there?" This time, I had my answer. I was going to throw that sucker of a ball up into the stands. I'd been known in the past to heave a football into the upper deck of Giants Stadium during warm-ups—just for the hell of it. When I got to the end zone, I started to fling the ball— but then I stopped. I had forgotten. I wasn't able to raise my arm above the level of my shoulder.

I played four or five tired games at the end of the season, and not a soul ever suggested that it made my season less or came from anything other than the flow of the action. That was my victory, that was my biggest award.

I was lucky to be on a Super Bowl team, but I've been lucky all my life. There's no guarantee that future seasons will be like that season or that the future will be anything like my past. I have two years and an option to go on my contract with the Giants. I will be thirty in 1989, and I can't envision playing beyond then. I won't play through the slow erosion of my abilities to the point where I'd be traded or cut—or forced to change my ways if I wanted to extend my career. I want to be the best. If I can't be, I'm gone. I won't play second best.

When I try to see the 1986 season, I try to keep it in perspective, to see it in terms of who I am rather than who others say I am. I wish I could speak out to fans and young people and say those things they would like to hear—but I can't. I can only be myself. That's the best I can ever urge on anyone else.

I had something to give back to Linda and my mom and pop and D'Fellas and Paul a lot of people from my hometown. I had plenty to play for.

When I was a kid, I was religious. I went to Sunday school, was a junior deacon in church, used to love listening to Bible stories in Sunday school. I've fallen away some in recent times, but strangely enough I've never stopped believing. My belief isn't like revealed truth written in stone where I no longer can be convinced of anything. Not someone who's stumbled as many times as I have.

I read Scripture aloud with the defensive line every week, I regularly talk to George Martin and to Father Moore, who runs our chapel, about improving my relationship with God. I still pray—as I did when I was a child—and I wear a cross. I believe deeply in God. And I tell Him, when I am alone, "I wish I were worthy of You, but I am not."

I am a wild man in a wild game. Sometimes, if I've really been watching my ass all week, I'll say to God in the tunnel before I go out on the field, "Okay, God, I did well this week, but it's time for that game again, got to go and be wild. I'll be back."

I believe God loves sinners and that he says even to people like me, "For now, you do what you have to do. Be wild. Kick butt on the field. Have a good time. But when this is over, you belong to Me."

I don't know when that will be.

But when that day comes, I'll be there.

Lawrence Taylor: Game-by-Game Statistics, 1981–86

Key: **T** = Tackles; **A** = Assists; **S** = Sacks; **Yds** = Yards lost

Opponent	T	A	S	Yds	Miscellaneous
		1981			
Philadelphia (L) 10–24	4	5	0		
Washington (W) 17–7	7	0	0		1 blocked pass
New Orleans (W) 20–7	3	1	0		
Dallas (L) 10–18	2	2	0		1 blocked pass
Green Bay (L) 14–27	3	6	1	8	
St. Louis (W) 34–14	2	2	1	9	
Seattle (W) 32–0	6	2	0.5	4.5	
Atlanta (W) 27–24 (OT)	7	2	0		3 blocked passes
Jets (L) 7–26	3	3	2	17	
Green Bay (L) 24–26	4	0	2	18	1 blocked pass
Washington (L) 30–27 (OT)	8	4	0		
Philadelphia (W) 20–10	4	2	0		
San Francisco (L) 10–17	3	3	0		
Rams (W) 10–7	3	2	1	6	interception
St. Louis (W) 20–10	3	3	2	24	1 blocked pass
Dallas (W) 13–10 (OT)	3	4	0		fumble recovery
		PLAYOFFS			
Philadelphia (W) 27–21	4	3	1	7	
San Francisco (L) 24–38	2	3	1	3	
Total reg. season	65	41	9.5	86.5	
Playoff totals	6	6	2	10	
Grand totals (18 games)	71	47	11.5	96.5	

Opponent	T	A	S	Yds	Miscellaneous
1982					
Atlanta (L) 14–16	1	7	1	10	
Green Bay (L) 19–27	3	3	1.5	15	fumble recovery

STRIKE CANCELS SEVEN WEEKS

Washington (L) 17–27	2	5	0		
Detroit (W) 13–6	3	0	1	9	97-yard TD interception
Houston (W) 17–14	2	0	1	14	
Philadelphia (W) 23–7	2	3	3	32	
Washington (L) 14–15	5	1	0		1 blocked pass
St. Louis (L) 21–24	4	0	0		
Philadelphia (W) 26–24	4	2	0		
Grand totals (9 games)	26	21	7.5	80	

Opponent	T	A	S	Yds	Miscellaneous
1983					
Rams (L) 6–16	7	2	0		2 fumble recoveries
Atlanta (W) 16–13 (OT)	9	0	0		
Dallas (L) 13–28	4	0	0		1 blocked pass
Green Bay (W) 27–3	4	2	0		1 blocked pass
San Diego (L) 34–41	4	2	0.5	4	interception; 1 blocked pass
Philadelphia (L) 13–17	7	3	0		
Kansas City (L) 17–38	2	7	0.5	3	1 blocked pass
St. Louis (T) 20–20	8	3	0.5	8	
Dallas (L) 20–38	6	1	1	9	
Detroit (L) 9–15	5	0	0		
Washington (L) 17–33	5	6	1	9	
Philadelphia (W) 23–0	3	0	1	3	
Raiders (L) 12–27	5	4	0		1 blocked pass
St. Louis (L) 6–10	1	4	1	9	1 blocked pass
Seattle (L) 12–17	6	2	0		1 blocked pass
Washington (L) 22–31	3	1	3	10	interception
Grand totals (16 games)	79	37	8.5	55	

Opponent	T	A	S	Yds	Miscellaneous
		1984			
Philadelphia (W) 28–27	5	1	1	2	
Dallas (W) 28–7	8	1	3	16	interception; fumble recovery
Washington (L) 14–30	4	4	0		
Tampa Bay (W) 17–14	6	0	4	33	
Rams (L) 12–33	5	1	0		1 blocked pass
San Francisco (L) 10–31	4	1	0		
Atlanta (W) 19–7	2	4	0		2 blocked passes
Philadelphia (L) 10–24	4	3	0		
Washington (W) 37–13	9	3	1	8	
Dallas (W) 19–7	4	1	0.5	4	1 blocked pass
Tampa Bay (L) 17–20	5	1	0		
St. Louis (W) 16–10	6	0	1	10	interception
Kansas City (W) 28–27	5	2	0		
Jets (W) 20–10	2	1	0		
St. Louis (L) 21–31	8	1	1	11	
New Orleans (L) 3–10	4	1	0		3 blocked passes
	PLAYOFFS				
Rams (W) 16–13	6	0	1	0	
San Francisco (L) 10–21	5	1	2	17	1 blocked pass
Total reg. season	81	25	11.5	84	
Playoff totals	11	1	3	17	
Grand totals (18 games)	92	26	14.5	101	

Opponent	T	A	S	Yds	Miscellaneous
		1985			
Philadelphia (W) 21–0	4	2	2.5	23.5	
Green Bay (L) 20–23	3	1	0.5	3	
St. Louis (W) 27–17	4	1	0		
Philadelphia (W) 16–10	6	4	0		
Dallas (L) 29–30	3	1	0		
Cincinnati (L) 30–35	2	2	1	3	
Washington (W) 17–3	11	0	2	23	
New Orleans (W) 21–13	5	1	1	9	
Tampa Bay (W) 22–20	3	2	0		
Rams (W) 24–19	5	3	0		
Washington (L) 21–23	11	0	2	9	fumble recovery
St. Louis (W) 34–3	4	0	2	18	1 blocked pass
Cleveland (L) 33–35	3	1	1	7	
Houston (W) 35–14	2	0	0.5	10	
Dallas (L) 21–28	2	0	0		
Pittsburgh (W) 28–10	3	1	0		
		PLAYOFFS			
San Francisco (W) 17–3	7	2	1	4	
Chicago (L) 0–21	8	2	0		
Total reg. season	71	19	12.5	105.5	
Playoff totals	15	4	1	4	
Grand totals (18 games)	86	23	13.5	109.5	

Opponent	T	A	S	Yds	Miscellaneous
		1986			
Dallas (L) 28–31	4	2	1.5	8	
San Diego (W) 20–7	2	2	0		
Raiders (W) 14–9	3	0	0		
New Orleans (W) 20–17	7	2	0		
St. Louis (W) 13–6	8	0	2	16	
Philadelphia (W) 35–3	11	2	4	25	
Seattle (L) 12–17	3	1	0		
Washington (W) 27–20	8	1	3	37	
Dallas (W) 17–14	3	5	1	2	
Philadelphia (W) 17–14	8	2	3	15	
Minnesota (W) 22–20	6	0	2	6	
Denver (W) 19–16	3	2	0		
San Francisco (W) 21–17	2	2	0		
Washington (W) 24–14	5	0	3	17	
St. Louis (W) 27–7	5	3	1	11	
Green Bay (W) 55–24	1	2	0		
		PLAYOFFS			
San Francisco (W) 49–3	0	2	0		34-yard TD interception
Washington (W) 17–0	2	3	0		
Denver (W) 39–20	4	1	0		
Total reg. season	79	24	20.5	137	
Playoff totals	6	6	0	0	
Grand totals (19 games)	85	30	20.5	137